Prospects of Life After Birth

Prospects of Life After Birth

Memoir in Poetry and Prose

David Hedges

Sweetbriar Press

Thanks to these publications in which the following poems made their first appearance: "Prospects of Life After Birth," and "How Mary Lou Moved," *Calapooya Collage;* "Down in Sullivan's Gulch," *Encore;* "Uncle Melvin's Folly," *Measure;* "Skipping Sunday School," "Disaster on Dead Man's Hill," and "The Eternal Years are Hers," *Verseweavers;* "Meeting Aunt Ovidia at Union Station," *Windfall;* "The Other Gang," *The Lyric;* "The Rose to Saint Louis," *Bellowing Ark;* "Sailor Jim and the World's Most Fantastic Hobo Shack," "The Barnum & Bailey Train," and "Immortal Prose," *Northwest Magazine;* "When Joe Drew Russia as a Class Assignment," *Poet Lore.*

Sweetbriar Press, P.O. Box 123, West Linn, OR 97068

Copies may be ordered at david.hedges.name/books

Layout, design, and typography by Andrew Hedges.

Front cover photo (1940) used with permission of Conway Bruno Studios. Back cover photo (2010) by Scottie Sterrett, at the Stonehenge War Memorial in the Columbia River Gorge.

ISBN 978-0-9658601-3-0

Printed in the United States of America.

I dedicate this book to my parents,
Dwight Sumner Hedges and Olive Ritan Hedges,
who gave me the freedom to explore.

Eyes Beyond Sight

Ah, love, let us be true
To one another!
—Matthew Arnold

As a child, on many a dream-tossed night
I crept from bed and stole down the hall
To the head of the stairway, hugging the wall
A church mouse shrinking from light

There, for a time, to curl up tight
Listening, blanket wrapped round like a shawl
To words spilled the way leaves fall
Watching through eyes beyond sight

As my mother, pacing in firelight
Pulled *Dover Beach* from fond recall
Swept up my father and held him in thrall
On the wings of a swan in flight.

Contents

Preface

One: Prospects of Life After Birth

Two: Disaster on Dead Man's Hill

Three: Curse of the Spider Woman

Four: The Rose to Saint Louis

Five: Chug-a-Lugging the Champ at the *Arsenic and Old Lace* Cast Party

Six: Battle of the Strippers

About the Author

Preface

"Return with us now to those thrilling days of yesteryear."

If you're of a certain age, you recognize these words as the introduction to *The Lone Ranger,* a radio show we "watched" weekly, using our imaginations to furnish the moving pictures.

Growing up in the 1940s and '50s, I was forced to use my imagination a lot. My parents didn't own a television set until 1954, by which time I was off to college.

But I never lacked for entertainment. In fact, as you'll soon discover from these pages, my life, from birth through the first half of my seventeenth year—the period covered in this book— is filled with adventure.

I should warn you, this book is not for everyone. I confess to being a narrative formalist. I tell stories in verse that's both rhythmical and rhymed.

At the same time, I don't consider myself a throwback to an age where formalism was all the rage. I'm not especially influenced by any one poet's style. I simply choose to paddle my canoe through still waters, staying out of the mainstream as much as possible, and writing whatever tickles my fancy.

I blame poet Laurence Pratt for my early bent. I was sailing along just fine, pouring myself into theater and jazz, when he walked into his classroom on the first day of my junior year at Lake Oswego High School, and, without so much as a how-do-you-do, began reciting *Beowulf* in Old English.

I was struck dumb. I seemed to understand this strange and thoroughly unfamiliar tongue, though probably it was more a case of recognizing inflections and patterns of speech.

In any event, it altered my path. Since my fifth year on the planet, I'd planned to become a paleontologist. Now, with Mr. Pratt as my mentor, I toyed with the idea of becoming a poet.

He submitted a poem of mine that was published, with special mention, in the National High School Poetry Anthology, and gifted me at graduation with one of his books of poems, in which he had written, "To David Hedges, who has shown skill in poetic composition." I was hooked.

I also blame my parents, both of whom wrote poetry during their high school and college years, and who exposed me to an extensive library that included works by and about poets from ancient Greece through the Modern era.

When the collection was divvied up among the three sons, I grabbed off, among other prizes, an utterly beautiful twelve-volume, leather-bound *Édition de Luxe* of the complete works of Alfred, Lord Tennyson, published in 1892. It took me a few years, but I read every volume, cover to cover.

In that respect, I also blame Tennyson, as well as Byron, Keats and Shelley, Edna St. Vincent Millay, and a slew of others, for drawing me into formalism.

This preference has limited my publication options, but as nice as it is, seeing my work in print is secondary to the thrill of conceiving a poem and bringing it to fruition.

It doubles my pleasure to start a poem and have the words shout out a particular form, sonnet and terza rima being two of my favorites. I also enjoy writing prose poems, and close this book with two prose pieces chronicling summers spent in the pea and wheat harvests of Eastern Oregon's Umatilla County.

I didn't set out to produce a "memoir in poetry and prose," but at a certain point I reviewed my oeuvre (a splendid term!) and realized just how often I had turned to experiences in my early years for inspiration.

I attended Oregon State College (now University) on a Navy scholarship, and did, after all, major in geology. Mom talked me into it, pointing out that I might need a skill to fall back on. As a result, I didn't take a single course with "poetry" in its title, though I did take writing courses, including one taught by Bernard Malamud. (I could tell you tales.)

In my sophomore year, the editor of the off-campus humor magazine bestowed on me the title of assistant editor. A year later, he left school and the *Beaver dam* was mine, all mine.

My interest in geology as a profession gradually slipped to zero, until, one term into my senior year and six months shy of a degree and a Navy commission, I dropped out and headed for Greenwich Village.

My New York adventures are chronicled in my chapbook, *A Funny Thing Happened on my Way to a Geology Degree* (Finishing Line Press, 2011).

I'm working on another couple of chapbooks that cover the gap between this book and *A Funny Thing,* and two full-length book manuscripts, one of them autobiographical. At 82, I'm beginning to feel some urgency to get it all out there.

I hope you enjoy reading my stories as much as I enjoyed living them, and writing them.

David Hedges
March, 2019

One:

Prospects of Life After Birth

Prospects of Life After Birth

Portland, Oregon, January 9, 1937

When I was born, demented by the drug this one nurse used
To keep me in the oven, snug, while old Doc Frisbee took
His ever-loving blue-eyed time, deformed when the forceps fused
My malleable skull a tiny bit because the O.B. book

Had failed to say a thing about a laid-back baby's birth
And I resisted—God, I fought! Who wouldn't start a scrap,
With room and board provided free, for all his world was worth,
When what he held could not be weighed or measured on a map?

It wasn't old Doc Frisbee's fault the night nurse pushed me back.
His trolley plowed to Halsey Street before the pulley froze,
And while he trekked the dozen blocks alone along the track
To Portland Sanitarium through wildly blowing snows,

I twice poked out as if to ask a favor, and the nurse
Reversed me with the flat of her hand pressed against my head,
Scolding my wide-eyed mother as the everlasting curse
Of her profession, how she could secure a post instead

In Daytime Dresses, Lingerie, Perfumes at Meier & Frank,
And should indeed be home in bed, letting her sweet dreams bloom.
Lo and behold, the Doc arrived and gave my bottom a spank,
Dangling me by the ankles while I wailed farewell to the womb,

Wondering who in creation dreamt this dreadful atmosphere,
The sickly cotton gowns and masks, the off-white tile floor,
The wrinkled rubber ether bag, the lights designed with fear
In mind by demons lurking just outside the O.R. door.

as told to me by my mother

A Teller of Tall Tales

I keep my childhood portrait close at hand.
It makes an honest man of me when fraud
And artifice advance their lotus-land

Temptations as the perfect path to God.
Those curly locks, those rosy cheeks, those eyes
Hand-tinted blue, a chin that seems to nod

Assent when I throw off my thin disguise
And rise as who I am, the good, the bad,
The ugly, all the in-betweens. Surprise

Is what I sometimes see, as if the lad
Has made a study of my closet's bones,
And, though my alibis are iron-clad,

Tsk-tsks and plays my ribs like xylophones.
I am a picnic basket full of me,
A fleet of small boats ballasted with stones

Afloat like bottles bobbing on the sea.
A child no more, yet not some churlish brute
Locked in his ways, I court hyperbole.

When I was five, my sense of sight acute,
I saw the leaders of the Axis fly
Low overhead, and I, in absolute

Control of all the universe, the sky
Above my house on Northeast Hancock Street
Included, ran inside, and with a cry

Of fright revealed what I had seen, replete
With details only I was privy to.
My mom, her voice, as always, firm yet sweet,

Said, "Hitler? Mussolini? Is this true?"
Thus forced to face reality, I said,
"No . . . only Mussolini." And I knew,

With superheated, sparkling, watershed
Elucidation, one day I'd become
A teller of tall tales, a fountainhead

Of modern myth. Though, as a high school chum
Scrawled in my yearbook, "Don't misunderstand,
Old friend, but you'd be splendid as a bum."

Down in Sullivan's Gulch

I wrench the clump of Johnson grass free
moments before the old switch engine
lurches back to life, wheezing.
With the right loft, the right twist of my wrist,
I can plant the grass deep in the stack
until pressure blows the soot black mass
sky high, and thick smoke drives engineer
and fireman down out of the cab, wide-eyed.

Thoughts swing to my first time on the rope,
my first plunge into billows of alien air
belched from the silver-painted throat
of the Portland Rose, Saint Louis bound—
the time I doubled Mackie's dare
by holding on with just one hand,
out through the fiery blast and back,
breathless, eyes tight against the sting
until at last I stood at the bank's trembling lip,
let go the rope, dropped to the soft dirt cupped
between the leaning fir tree's twisted roots
and laughed to tears, while Mackie, hands
stuffed in pockets, scuffed his heels
in the thick dust, studying defeat.

The engine hisses, stutters, spits
steam jets along the polished rails
and down the raised bed of crushed rock
and creosote-coated ties, splashing
the tar-black gravel by the water tank,
and spins its wheels for the gandy dancers
lounging by the tool shed, as if headed
for the stretch of track that hugs the Columbia

River like a snake, up the Gorge where it
hauled a hundred freight cars in its glory days.
Back and forth, using both hands,
I swing the jumbo clump of Johnson grass,
letting go, betting last week's allowance,
a buffalo nickel, on the twist of my wrist.

The Iceman

Jingling in time with the clip-clop
of the dappled gray horse's hooves,
the brass bell attached to the worn leather
harness brought every kid on Hancock Street
running on a hot summer afternoon, knowing
the familiar weathered wood ice wagon
was about to round the corner at 32nd Avenue
and pop into sight. This meant slivers, chips,
even chunks were ours as the iceman worked
his magic, shaping a block to fit an icebox.

We had an older model Sears & Roebuck
out on the back porch, with a green body
and three cream colored doors with nickel-
plated hinges worn through enough to show
the brass beneath. When the iceman grabbed
the block with his tongs and hefted it onto
his shoulder, I stayed on his heels around
the house till he reached the back steps, then
held the screen door open, my way of saying
thanks for chipping me off all those slivers.

Then one sad day, without consulting me,
Mom and Dad bought a GE refrigerator.
It looked like a robot, or a space alien
from the cover of a science fiction pulp,
its monitor perched on top like a weird head.
I was distraught. Did they not know what
this meant to every kid on Hancock Street?
I cried my eyes out. No more horse-drawn
wagon. No more iceman. No more ice.

At Five I Found My First True Love

A red bug with six black legs
and funny fernlike feelers
lumbers out of my forearm forest
and stumbles about in the clearing.
I contemplate my wrist,
the white line tracing the time
I tried flooding the tin sandbox
behind my Hancock Street home,
juggling Mason jars up steep
basement steps until glass shattered,
dust swirled, tears flowed, and there,
hair glowing in the noon sun,
stood the nurse next door.
She stopped the blood, clamped
the wound closed, soothed my fears
with her flow of easy words,
her mystic whispers. Together,
we cultivated Victory Garden corn,
peas, tomatoes, lettuce, beans.
When she went off to war, I lay
awake nights, counting the stars
piercing my blackout blinds,
wondering if she still loved me.
The red bug with six black legs
flies away, waving its feelers.

Mackie's Bad Day at the Circus

We hatched a plot: We show up early, hang
Around while people go about their work,
Enjoy the hustle-bustle, watch the gang

Of roustabouts flex muscles as they jerk
The heavy ropes that raise the tents, explore
The cages where the cats are kept, and lurk

In shadows so the plainclothes dicks ignore
Two kids intent on sneaking in. At first
We blended fine—but fate had plans in store.

A big man with two wooden buckets burst
Our bubble: "How would you scamps like to earn
Free passes while you satisfy the thirst

Of our grand pachyderms? Great chance to learn
About these wondrous creatures. Here, I'll show
You what to do." This was a super turn

For me, but Mackie seemed a little slow
To go along, and let his bucket drag.
I never thought I'd ever get to know

Real elephants! I couldn't wait to brag
To friends how I could feel their breath! But by
My seventh bucket I began to sag.

My arms and shoulders hurt, my mouth was dry.
Mackie, by this time, had taken off,
Giving me a flimsy alibi.

I hobbled back and forth, from water trough
To pump, on wobbly legs, until the boss
Appeared and set my bucket down. "I doff

My hat to you, young sir! I'm at a loss
To thank you for your stamina, your grit.
How would you like a special seat across

The big top where the dignitaries sit?"
A dream come true—the colors and the lights!
The costumed elephants performed a skit.

The trapeze artists glittered in their tights.
The clown car made me laugh so hard I cried.
I took it all in—swallowed sounds and sights—

Until, beyond the center ring, I spied
A painful scene that gave my heart a pang:
Mackie, plainclothes dicks on either side.

Skipping Sunday School

I learned more about God
in the front seat of my family's
'34 Plymouth four door sedan
than I ever did in Sunday School,
which I skipped religiously
while the folks absorbed their
sermon, sang their hymns, recited
the Lord's Prayer and Benediction,
and dropped their little white
envelope in the deep dish
making its way from pew to pew
in the stone and stained glass splendor
of Westminster Presbyterian Church.
Bach, Beethoven and Brahms
were my teachers, Mozart
and Vivaldi, as The Firestone Hour
wrapped me in the flowing robes
of fiery gods, oblivious to sunlight
streaming through gold leaves
on the horse chestnut trees lining
16th Avenue, the purrs and putts
of passing cars, immersed
in the mathematics of the soul,
wondering how a war could rage
while the radio played a Chopin polonaise.

Meeting Aunt Ovidia at Union Station

A sailor, a white-hat like my Uncle Hank,
hugs a woman so tight I can't see daylight
between them. His hands climb her back, lift
her flimsy skirt, show straight-seamed nylons
clipped to garters on a girdle, like the ones
in the Sears & Roebuck catalogue in Uncle
Melvin's outhouse on the Estacada farm.

A Marine with rows of ribbons on his chest
grabs a woman with an upswept hair-do
and sweeps her off her feet, setting off squeals
that pierce the hubbub like an air raid siren.
She swings bare legs, longer than I am tall
between pink-pantied bottom and rolled-down
bobby sox, and wraps them around his waist.

A blue balloon, left over from some welcome
home, hovers in the haze midway between tile
floor and vaulted ceiling, wrinkled like a prune,
the string too high for me to reach. Headlines
at the blind man's news and tobacco stand
shout how well the war in Europe is going,
how the boys should all be home by Christmas.

When Aunt Ovidia's train finally arrives, Nana
will lead me through the gray doors with chips
showing six or seven shades of layered paint,
grimy window panes inset with chicken wire,
brightwork polished by a million hands, along
the platform where green baggage carts weave
in and out, to greet her in a great hiss of steam.

Nana talks about how Ovidia, prettiest among
the seven sisters, envy of all the wallflowers,
kept a dozen suitors dangling like ripe plums
until one by one they dropped. She wed too late
to have children. Gedward died in the pandemic.
Now she makes the rounds by rail, visiting kin
for a month, so as not to wear thin her invitation.

She carries what little is left of her life packed
in a pair of steamer trunks. Lace collars, kid
gloves, high-button shoes, hats with black veils.
The train stops. Steps drop. Nana, hands dead
ahead as in prayer, plows like a cowcatcher
through the chaos of carts and porters. In a great
hiss of steam, I feel a prickly peck on my cheek.

Uncle Melvin's Folly

Townspeople said he did the Devil's work.
God-fearing Christians plowed and tilled the soil
Six days a week, then put aside their toil
To pray for their eternal souls. "Berserk!"
They shouted, and "Idolater!" His quirk,
The dream his next-door neighbors sought to spoil
By stealth, his burning drive to drill for oil
Where none was known, caused steady folk to jerk.
Night after night he jacked the heavy stones
Dumped in his well, his block-and-tackle powered
By tandem mules. Night after night he drilled
A few feet further till his aching bones
Told him to quit. So what if Brothers glowered
And Sisters sneered? God's will, he'd be fulfilled.

Aunt Agnes shared his hopes and nursed his pains
With stoicism. Peace of mind and strife
Played hopscotch on the sidewalks of her life.
Her Melvin was a man who used his brains
In concert with his hands. He broke the chains
Binding him to chores. Oil dripped from her knife
At the pond, and (not because she was his wife)
She nodded at the rings, the rainbow stains.
She thought of Jörgensen, whose Wireless claim
Was jumped, whose props were knocked from under
Him. They languished in the Philippines,
Weathered the insurrection. Nobel fame
Aside, their fortune was denied. Thunder-
Struck, they were reduced to eating beans.

Agnes cooked and washed and milked the cow
While Melvin plowed by day and slogged the night
Clearing out his well by lantern light
And drilling a few feet more. She wondered how
She would have handled wealth if now
She was the widow of a famous man so bright
He dodged the great Marconi's oversight
Without a shot being fired across his bow.
For fifty years she kept her man abeam
Until at ninety-six, while pounding nails
In shingles on the roof, he dropped, his dream
Fulfilled, a Pharaoh carried up the Nile
Reclined on lion skins and ermine tails.
It was the only time she saw him smile.

When Joe Jumped from the Upstairs Window

Mom and Dad had told Joe to go to bed
until they were blue in the face. He balked—
the party was going strong—so they locked
the door at the head of the stairs instead.
Preferring the company of adults
to that of kids his own age, all the more
because he was able to hold the floor
on a wide range of topics while insults
and babble were all most kids could handle,
he climbed out and stood on the window ledge.
Using his nightie as a parachute,
he leaped, exposing us all to scandal,
dropped like a rock to the boxwood hedge
between house and walk, gave me a salute,

and limped to the front porch. I heard the bell
through the crack under the door, and the voice
of Uncle Hank, who always threw a choice
word or two into the pot, this time, "Hell
if it ain't the brat!" to peals of laughter
from the other guests, and rounds of applause
as Joe recounted, blow by blow, to Ahs
and Ohs, his perilous flight. And after
the last guest left, after Joe's last story
laid 'em in the aisles, knocked 'em from their chairs,
hit 'em on their funny bones, made 'em weep,
euphoria sweeping him to glory
beyond his dreams, Dad carried him upstairs
and tucked him gently into bed, asleep.

When Joe Played Doctor and Got in Dutch

It was a splendid gift for one with heart,
complete with candy pills and stethoscope,
and Joe made all assembled breathe with hope
for the younger generation, the part
about how seeds planted in fertile minds
bloom as tomorrow's brainchildren. He donned
his cap and gown as one who'd formed a bond
with destiny, one of those wondrous kinds
of prodigies famed in biographies
for skipping the formalities. He shone
in his own eyes as a healer whose skills
were unsurpassed in the annals of disease
control. The next day, he set out to hone
his proficiency with medical drills.

He enlisted a nurse from the next block
and set up his kit at the curb. Among
the sundry items he arrayed were tongue
depressors, cotton swabs, a tomahawk
for tapping knees, and rubber gloves. He'd pick
on every little kid who passed, whose cure
was quick. His eye popped from the aperture
of his physician's mirror: "Write down sick,"
he'd tell Nurse Nancy, who barely knew how
to spell her own name. Nurse Nancy's brother,
who was three, put an end to Joe's career.
His sister pinned him down. He shouted "Ow!"
and ran screaming home to tell their mother.
(Joe had stuck an otoscope in his ear.)

Mom kept from smiling as Nurse Nancy's mom
droned on. She pretended she had dirty chores
she couldn't duck, and repeated, "My door's
always open to a neighbor," to calm
the waters. Nancy's mom refused to buy
stock in Mom's notion that Joe had "a need
inspired by a keen desire to succeed,"
a praiseworthy trait, or that "those with high
hopes for their offspring set them free." Then
the green-eyed monster reared its ugly head.
"Nancy will reign as Rose Festival Queen,
attend the U of O, and marry when
a boy with wealthy parents, both well-bred,
proposes to Nancy's dad. He'll be clean

and well-mannered, won't smoke, or drink liquor,
or stay out late at night." She left, restored
to her former happy state, while Mom, bored
stiff, burst out laughing. "There's nothing thicker
than some people's heads!" When Joe and I
popped from under the kitchen table, we
all had a good chuckle. Then Mom told me
to go pick up my room, which meant, "Go fly
a kite while Joe and I discuss fateful
matters of global import." I, all ears,
peeked through the crack behind the door as she
explained how some people can seem hateful
when they have the best intentions. Joe's tears
freshened an old expression, "Let it be!"

He retired his kit the way he buried
stray cats run over in the street, with rites
conducted out-of-doors by the moonlight's
soft glow. I dug the hole, and he carried
the body, the black valise with *M.D.*
stamped on either side, shrouded by the Stars
and Stripes. He might as well have flown to Mars
as try to "do the doctor thing," when he
had "no higher moral guide than his peers,"
who, obviously, at that tender age,
had "scant conception of the lures of life,"
according to Nancy's mother, whose fears
of bogeymen put Nancy in a cage,
alone, a perfect stranger's model wife.

Watching Sheet Lightning from Maryanne Davenport's Front Porch

Dark clouds, gunmetal gray, smother the sky
above the peaked roofs across Schuyler Street.
Thunder rumbles south to north like a hundred
kettledrums pounded with fists, a cannonade.

The six of us kids sit wide-eyed on the top step,
holding hands, shouting the names of sky gods,
shrieking with glee every time sheet lightning
sweeps west to east like wildfire in a stiff wind.

The clouds burst overhead—raindrops splatter
the porch, dance on the roofs across the street.
Gutters overflow, rivers rage down driveways.
Dumbstruck, we jump up, huddle by the door.

The Other Gang

When lazy days were long on Hancock Street,
Hours turned round, minutes strung like beads,
We cornered dragons in their lairs and beat
The pants off pirates with our daring deeds.
We fashioned forts in thickets Superman
Could not see into, swung hands-free from trees,
And when the sun was low, played kick-the-can
Or hide-and-seek or mother-may-I-please.
I knew this perfect world we shared would stay
A place of make-believe and let's pretend,
But on toward fall my family moved away.
Leaves fell, snow came, in time I found a friend.
Now when I draw the faded photos out
The magic rises like a waterspout.

Two:

Disaster on Dead Man's Hill

Disaster on Dead Man's Hill

Charlie Withers told me about the time
he showed off for his older brother Pete by riding
his bike up Dead Man's Hill and halfway up
a pedal flew off and the part that held the pedal on
sliced open an artery and if Pete hadn't been there
they would have renamed it Dead *Boy's* Hill.

I tell the story to Nicky Warner as he rides
down Dead Man's Hill on top of eight bundles
of newspapers for the Alameda School Paper
Drive late on the last day naturally and the Radio
Flyer wobbling on its wheels and me putting
a shoulder to the bundles and trying to steer.

I want Nicky to know I'm there for him in case
something bad happens and it's still called Dead
Man's Hill and nothing on the wagon is sharp
and the whole thing starts to tip and strings pop
and papers pour over the walk and skitter into the street
and Nicky flips and lands on his hands and knees.

I tell Nicky he's lucky to be alive and with no
broken bones and to hurry and help gather papers
and tears flow down his cheeks and dribble off his chin
and he holds out his hands and shows me his knees
and streetlights pop on as he hobbles up the hill
and I deliver four bundles just under the deadline.

Second Prize Binge

Mom got her Cub Scout Den to build a float
Of blossoms for the Junior Rose Parade,
Washington crossing the Delaware in a boat,
Chicken wire with blooms of every shade.
I took on the task of finding flowers.
I knew where they grew—I'd snipped my share,
A dozen here and there, from back-yard bowers,
Border beds, and sold them for a prayer.
Joe played Washington and got to ride
In costume, showering the crowd with waves
And smiles, bestowing kisses on the side,
While the other Cubs and I played galley slaves.
We divvied sixteen bucks—two dollars each—
And blew it in an afternoon at Jantzen Beach.

When Joe Joined the Northeast Portland Youth Orchestra

The whole idea was Nana's. She thought
Joe, being first-born, should learn how to play
an instrument. She went to Sherman Clay,
draining the options dry before she bought
The Violin. She then called Eichenlaub,
a fabled teacher, one whose wide renown
was heightened by his lofty fees. Downtown
Joe went each week, transferring to the Nob
Hill trolley at Third and Taylor, his case
carried under his arm, machine-gun style,
pretending he was Babyface Malone
running numbers to Bugsy Siegel's place,
kissing off the coppers on his heels while
shaking the goons of rival Al Capone,

fantastic footwork for a bantamweight.
"Ten-oh-two!" moaned Eichenlaub, who had told
Joe to be there on the dot. He would scold
in Yiddish, but always, Joe arrived late,
his ready alibi contrived: "Golly,
the Jackson Tower clock must be broken!"
or "Gee, I misplaced my silly token!"
or "Wow, a car broadsided my trolley!"
Always, Eichenlaub would brush off Joe's tall
tale with a wave, eyes raised as if saying,
"Why me?" while betraying a tender streak,
recalling his own lackadaisical
youth. His major concern was Joe's playing,
which improved very slowly from one week

to the next; he accused Joe of shirking
his responsibility: "Practice!" he'd
implore, and Joe would pretend to bleed
all over, mowed down by mobsters lurking
in the shadows. (To tell the truth, he *did*
practice—all the time, judged by complaints
from both next door neighbors, themselves no saints
in the noise department.) Not one to kid
around, Eichenlaub drove Joe up and down
the scales, clapping his hands to his ears each
time Joe skipped a fret, or turned a note sour.
His was a face with a permanent frown.
Joe jumped for joy when a session would screech
to a halt, freed, by the strike of the hour,

to hurry home and grab his baseball glove.
Not that he wasn't musically inclined:
Great-grandpa Bray had seen his name enshrined
as a musical pioneer, his love
so great he mastered every instrument,
led bands and orchestras, composed, and taught
his generation's Joes. Mom had a shot
at a concert career, which might have meant
fame and fortune. She performed *Liebestraum*
on a Steinway baby grand on the stage
of Portland Civic Auditorium
before the graduating classes from
all the high schools, the applause a gauge
of her proficiency. A *Te Deum*

was followed by the announcement that she
got to keep the baby grand as a gift
from Nana and Mister Ritan, whose thrift
accounted for his wealth. Joe's apathy
had more to do with his burning desire
to play the saxophone, and emulate
the virtuosity of all the great
jazz artists of the age. His heart afire
in the dark, he'd listen to his short wave
set, and pick up jazz broadcasts live from New
York and Kansas City, after midnight,
pressing headphones to his ears. "Brother Dave!"
he'd say, "I heard *My One And Only You*
by Ben Webster, clear as a bell!" The light

of Joe's life lay away from the fiddle,
but Eichenlaub pushed him down that dark path,
driven by Nana's dough and his own wrath
over Joe's slow progress. He would twiddle
his thumbs, and tweak his manicured goatee
throughout the lesson, goading Joe because
"Eichenlaub's pupils play in orchestras
across the land, and I intend to see
you in one too!" He made it his mission
to find Joe a home in a local band
of young musicians. Swallowing his pride,
he got rival Schnable to audition
Joe for Northeast Orchestra. "I'll demand
a chair!" he swore, swaying from side to side.

You should have heard the muffled shouts, the things
said, when Eichenlaub flung Joe at Schnable.
Right away they began to squabble
over Joe's proper place among the strings.
Joe walked the dog between "Second!" and "First!"
assuming "I Don't Know!" was on cello,
noting how Schnable bobbed like Costello.
He was Eichenlaub's "Best!" or Schnable's "Worst!"—
up or down, depending on which one swung
the yo-yo. Eichenlaub had never faced
the prospect of a pupil forced to sit
with second fiddles: "Joe is too high-strung
to saw away at chords! I'll be disgraced!
He'll be bored!" Schnable would have none of it

till Eichenlaub proposed a compromise:
"Make him the *last* of the first violins,
and may fortune's tide wash away your sins."
Joe took his seat, far from Schnable's reprise
of Eichenlaub's harping on fumbled frets.
Free to pluck a stray note, or slur a phrase,
he mucked about and made clean getaways
through rhapsodies and over minuets,
galloping lickety-split. Mom and Dad
took Nana and me to opening night
of the May Day concert at Grant High School;
they rendered *Over the Rainbow*. "Egad!"
Joe thundered at the end. He'd done it right,
sparing Eichenlaub Schnable's ridicule.

When Joe Stole the Show
at Portland Junior Civic Theatre

Auditions were tough, but Joe got the part,
the woodsman in *Little Red Riding Hood*
who whacks the wolf with his ax. Little good
the tool did him at the end, but let's start
with the scene where the wolf, in Grandma's gown,
convinces Red to shed her fear of eyes,
ears, nose and teeth, to expect a surprise
soon, and to put her picnic basket down.
That's how the script read, but Joe wrote a brand
new version. He ran on, pranced to center
stage, and realized—*"Oops!"*—the wolf had four
more lines. Beneath the floor, flashlight in hand,
the prompter stage-whispered, "You don't enter
yet!" Joe said *"Oh!"* and ran back out the door.

Maybe it was just a case of first-night
jitters. Maybe somebody backstage blew
in his ear, and he viewed it as a cue.
Whatever the cause, he saw the green light
wink on, threw his transmission into first
gear, and gave it the gas. The rafters flung
laughter back. A flashing neon sign hung
over my bowed head: *Joe's brother!* The worst
awaited; right then, writhing in mortal
shame, like Lillian Gish in a blizzard,
I'd struck rock bottom. Still, the great guffaw
reminded me of Frank Morgan's chortle
as Professor Marvel in *The Wizard
of Oz,* accepting of a minor flaw,

so I straightened up, determined to see
Joe through his big scene, and lead the acclaim
when the wolf bit the dust. I overcame
the flaming arrows of catastrophe—
what more could happen? When Joe reappeared,
this time accompanied by his merry band
of wood-choppers, cardboard axes in hand,
a strange smile split his face. Just as I feared,
he gazed across the apron, past the pit,
into the hearts of his adoring fans.
The wolf, upstaged twice now, rushed to bite
Joe, just as Joe hefted his broad-ax. It
decked the poor wolf, whose fellow thespians,
including Red, carried him off, stage right,

while Joe took his bows and showered kisses
on the balcony, and the frazzled stage
manager dropped the curtain. (Let's engage
in a fantasy: The curtain misses
Joe by inches, and he's left standing, proud
as punch, out in front before the footlights,
where rosebuds meant for Red fly at his tights
and tunic. Outside the stage door, a crowd
of worshipers waits . . . .) The first curtain call
produced a bedlam better than The Three
Stooges, with the wolf, still woozy, reeling
like Larry and Curly Joe, off the wall,
right after Moe knocks their noggins, the key
player, Red, distraught at the scene-stealing,

pouring mock tears out by the bucket load,
and the woodsmen, showing their tender side,
flitting between the two like elves astride
broomstick horses, knock-kneed and pigeon-toed,
steadying the wolf, and drying Red's eyes.
Joe did stand proud—the King of Siam
slouched, next to him. He was a happy clam,
gathering rosebuds, kissing butterflies,
just as I'd imagined, except the part
about the rosebuds, with a nod to *Let's*
Pretend. And butterflies notwithstanding,
he kissed every star in the sky. His heart
lifted off, his moon cheeks blazed like comets.
Nothing could eclipse his happy landing!

The Pee Pond

Halfway up Dead Man's Hill
on the public walk's steep stairs,
I stepped onto a narrow terrace,
pushed aside flowering vines, parted
spindly weeds, and peered into
a small green grotto in a stone wall
I'd never noticed before. An oval
goldfish pond appeared. I took a stick
to the thick mat of scum to see if any
fish still lived there. Finding none,
I unbuttoned my fly and peed.

Dad had told me people living
in the city don't pee out of doors,
but here I stood, free as a bird
flying overhead, peeing wherever
it pleased. I kept the Pee Pond a secret
for weeks, sneaking away from kids
trudging up Dead Man's Hill,
until I had to tell someone. My best
friend Gene looked over both
shoulders, laughed, and let loose.
Soon the whole school knew.
I quit when I had to stand in line.

"Do You Want to Go to Heaven?"

The man who reached inside his winter coat
Could not have known the terror in my bones,
The crush of fingers clutching at my throat,
The knife, the pool of blood, my dying groans—
For here it was, July, and hot to boot,
And I, at nine years old, was steeped in lore
Of pirates hacking limbs to gain their loot,
And sheiks whose daggers drenched the sands with gore.
He spoke no more and made no further move
But stood as if his tower had lost its clock,
While I, my needle in a static groove,
Went round and round until, unlocked from shock,
I bolted. "Wait!" he cried, his voice a sword,
"I am the light of the world, sayeth the Lord!"

Saturday Matinee at the Blue Mouse

Every Saturday morning, without fail,
I'd make a beeline for the trolley track
On Regents Drive and put my ear to the rail

Until I heard the familiar clickety-clack
Of the elegant old-time car I always caught,
Not like the squatty modern types. I'd pack

A bag of snacks, and plan to play a lot
Of games at the Penny Arcade on Fourth, to kill
Some time. The arcade was a melting pot

Of characters. I'd more than drink my fill
Of people-watching while I tried to keep
My car on the moving road, or honed my skill

At dropping a claw on a worthless prize, a cheap
Stuffed animal or such, or tried to get
The better of the ancient hand-cranked peep

Show that was rigged to make a body sweat
Flipping the cards, but always quit before
The promised naked lady popped. (I'd fret,

But pay to play again.) Then out the door
I'd fly, and up the street. I had a knack
For making lights. The Blue Mouse was in store!

They played *Animal Crackers* and *Duck Soup* back
To back, opening Groucho's bag of tricks,
The specs, the eyebrow-makeup moustache, black

Swallowtail coat, cigars, hot licks
Basting Margaret Dumont like a roast
On a spit in all seven of their flicks.

She was like kin to him. He liked to boast
She was "the Fifth Marx Brother" to avert
The hint of hanky-panky. He'd be toast

If Hedda Hopper served him for dessert
Or Walter Winchell bounced him like a ball
From coast to coast. Besides (to dig some dirt)

He gets his kicks from chicks, is prone to fall
For dames as phony as a winter night
Is long. I laugh to tears at Captain Spal-

Ding, roar at Kornblow, broadcast my delight
When shyster lawyer Rufus Firefly, an elf,
Flitters, crouched and striding, into sight.

And then there's Charlie Chaplin, playing himself,
Seeking refuge from an Arctic gale
In a ramshackle shack, the kitchen shelf

As bare as Old Mother Hubbard's, his humble goal
Boiling his high-topped shoes to soften the leather,
Picking out the nails like bones from sole

Fillets, oblivious to wind and weather.
Extras add their flavors to the stews—
Kornblow's femme fatale festooned in feathers

Proof enough. Buck Rogers puts the screws
To Martians speeding over crusty borax
Desert roads in cracker boxes whose

Synthetic rubber tires leave treaded tracks.
Mae West and W.C. Fields throw away
Their scripts and ad lib, vying to see who cracks

Up first. And Buster Keaton doesn't say
A word but makes me howl—the holy grail,
Horseplay as the order of the day!

The Voice of Lucky Beaver Baseball

Summer of 1945

Rollie Truitt was his name, the Voice
of Lucky Beaver Baseball. And what a voice
it was, winding to a fever pitch when Ad
Liska fanned the batters one-two-three,
or Rupert Thompson rapped a bases-loaded
three-and-two inside fast ball straight
into the left field bleachers, fans hollering
to high heaven. I hung out behind the press
box at home games, and glued myself to
a radio set for out-of-town games. Rollie
was as much a hero to me as Ted Gullic
with his fabled bat, or Johnny O'Neill, who
covered short field like a whirling dervish.

Here I was, a rookie member of the Knot Hole
Gang, a green kid with a wrinkle-free card,
lounging like a pro with the older boys on
the Vaughan Street Ballpark's 18th Avenue
boards, when out of the blue I was picked
to sit at Rollie's side for a playoff game, two
weeks shy of a miracle shot at the Pacific Coast
League pennant in the most fantastic season
Lucky Beaver Baseball had seen since 1906!

The big hero that day was not Charlie English,
who sparked a triple play from second base,
or All-Star catcher Roy Easterwood, who
caught foul tips as if they were warm-up
pitches—it was Rollie, who invited me,
of all his fans, to the KWJJ studio at Oaks Park
for the next away game. It was pure magic.

The telegraph, a black tin box that sounded
like a cross between a machine gun and a steam
locomotive on a steep downgrade, fed Rollie
a steady stream of copy that he read as if he
were right there in the ballpark, soaking up
the excitement. A bat connected—he clucked
his tongue and a hollow knock soared out over
the airwaves. He stuck a finger in his cheek,
turned from the mike and popped off a base hit.
Smacked his palm with a fist for a call strike.
Breathed fire into a slick bit of footwork
by Easterwood at the plate. Clapped a hand
to his mouth, echoing the roar of the crowd.
My scalp tingled—I knew the score.
Rollie's secret was safe with me.

Door to Door on Alameda Drive

The ad on the back cover of the Captain Marvel comic
said "Win Valuable Prizes!," an irresistible invitation
to one with aspirations like mine, to make a quick buck,
beat all comers, and wind up wearing the Spring Shoes
I could see propelling me up and down Alameda Drive.

Up and down Alameda Drive I trudged with my packets
of flower seeds tucked tightly into slots in the cardboard
box I could barely carry. Everybody bought one or two,
praising my enterprise. At a penny a packet, not exactly
a fortune. I never won the shoes. Probably nobody did.

Undaunted, I clipped another coupon and found myself
back on the beat, this time with little tins of burn salve
in a more manageable box. Sales were few and I earned
more blisters than bucks. But I learned to rattle off facts
machine-gun fashion: "Most accidents happen at home!"

From there it was a short hop to Christmas cards, where
all I carried was a sample book, a pen, and a pad of order
forms. Until the morning I woke to find huge cardboard
boxes stacked on the porch of my Hamblet Street home.
The driver tapped his foot while I labored over my name.

The folks were amazed. Three hundred orders to deliver,
and Thanksgiving a few days away. Bundled up in jacket,
hat, and mittens, clutching the handle of my Radio Flyer
wagon, I labored up and down Alameda Drive, stopping
at every second or third home, then back for another load.

Every time I pulled away from the steps, Mom drew aside the drape and peeked from hiding. Or so she thought, my keen eyes tuned to the slightest movement. It never dawned on me to ask for help. I had a daring scheme up my sleeve. Nobody knew what I intended, and only I could pull it off.

For over a year, I ate nothing for breakfast but Wheat Chex when I had a choice, and urged brothers Joe and Cap to do the same. At the mention of Wheaties, Cheerios, Shredded Wheat, I beat the drum for Wheat Chex and drowned it out, citing first-hand knowledge of "the many uses Wheat Chex

have, from after-school snacks to party mixes where they're baked with pretzel sticks and nuts." I promoted the stuff right and left. I fed it to the birds. The blue jays bit. I tried the cat. No way. The next-door-neighbor's Irish setter ate his share. I saved just enough box tops to make my dream come true.

The agony came when I sent the box tops off, along with my hard-earned bucks, to the Ralston-Purina Company. I waited and waited as Christmas drew closer and closer. When Mom asked me why I no longer ate Wheat Chex, I lied and said I'd developed a taste for Kix. Soon the big day was a week away.

Christmas Eve morning found me hanging out by the window in the living room, trying to keep suspicions down by telling everybody Gene might drop by, so nobody would notice when I bolted out the front door to greet the parcel post truck. The same driver tapped his foot while I labored over my name.

The folks were amazed. Always before, they'd turned us kids loose in the five-and-dime on Northeast Broadway with a few bucks to spend on everybody. We would agonize for hours on end over our limited choices before plunking our money down, relieved. This time, not even Joe and Cap knew what was up.

"Such an enormous box," said Mom. "And so heavy," said Dad. "It's from the three of us," said I, while Joe and Cap gawked. They knew I'd bought the present for the folks, and they had kicked in the couple of bucks they'd have spent, but I hadn't spilled the beans. The glitter knocked everybody for a loop.

A set of silver-plated dinnerware, complete with butter knives and gravy ladle. Everything but napkin rings and oyster forks, since we had Grandma's sterling silver napkin rings and never ate oysters except in stew. Besides, I'd have needed more box tops than I could eat Wheat Chex if I'd counted on the works.

Everybody laughed around the tree. Colored lights sparkled in eyes overflowing with oceans of love, a payoff worthy of my monumental effort. There was no settling for second best, no getting by half-baked. I wanted this more than a real bike. As Nana liked to say, "The more you give, the more you get."

I got my bike and took right off, wobbling on training wheels up and down Alameda Drive like a young Lawrence of Arabia on his stallion, waving to everybody I knew, which was every last living soul. Whole families stepped outside and wished me "Merry Christmas!," having seen me struggle past the other way.

I learned I had a firm client base when scores of Wheat Chex eaters up and down Alameda Drive told me they would have doubled consumption to speed me toward my goal, if they'd known. Those who welcomed my face at their doors said they'd buy a bridge from me because, by George, my word was good.

Like a self-fulfilling prophesy, time and again an entity perches on my shoulder when I fudge the truth or take it through a taffy pull. Nothing so dramatic as an angel in a white robe and shiny halo debating a devil in red tights with horns and pitchfork, like in the movies, but faces that keeps me honest without speaking.

The Watchbird watching me bears features of all the faces known
from my treks up and down Alameda Drive, going door to door.
Call it what you will, a built-in support group, fans in the stands,
an extended family, the village they say it takes to raise a child, I
was sheltered from storms of my own devising, and from outside.

When I was eleven and we moved to the country, Hamblet Street
and Alameda Drive went along, tucked away like Nana's old lace
handkerchiefs, weightless, more precious than gold. Sometimes I
bring them out for no reason. Sometimes they beckon with a soft
voice, inviting the light of day. Always I handle them with care.

Three:

Curse of the Spider Woman

Curse of the Spider Woman

It started when Nana took me and Joe to see
the Saturday matinee at the Irvington Theater.
Snow White and the Seven Dwarfs was billed
as family fare, a fairy tale. To me, being six,
the Queen was real. I cringed when she morphed
into a hideous witch who brewed poison by light
from a candle spilling wax on a human skull
with nasty rats popping from its eyeholes.

But the Queen paled beside what came next.
Sherlock Holmes and The Spider Woman, which
showed a deadly spider guided by the beam
from a penlight—out the vent, down the wall,
up the bedspread, onto the pillow, up the neck
to just behind the woman's ear—cut to black!
I died every night for weeks as spiders crept
across the floor, or dropped from the ceiling.

Nana, not one to waste a dime on a double bill
and not stay to see the second feature, lost all
her late husband's money in the Crash of '29
when his friends descended, clutching shares
guaranteed to boost her wealth. "Five percent
is all you pay!" they said, planting their hooks
a month before Black Thursday reeled her in
and Black Monday clubbed her like a salmon.

When we moved to the country, I packed my
fear of spiders along with my rock collection,
comic books, and baseball gloves. All went fine
until I stepped inside the vacant chicken house.
Webs hung everywhere, draped from rafters
and beams, strung between uprights, drawn like
cat's-cradles crisscrossing windows and doors.
Orb webs, sheet webs, funnel webs, cobwebs.

But the chicken house on a moonless midnight
was the only place for me to face a demon worse
than the evil Queen. Dying didn't seem as bad
as living with the fear of death. I crept from bed
and down the stairs without a sound, holding my
breath until I reached the door. From there I felt
my way, first to the old fir tree, then to the well,
then to the chicken house door, where I froze.

Dad had stored some steamer trunks inside
so the doorway was clear. I inched forward,
arms outstretched, unable to see the colossal
cobweb about to envelop my head. Next day
I plucked a black-and-yellow garden spider
from the fence, let it run down my forearm to
my fingertips, and dangle by a thread before
I put it back. The curse was lifted. I was free.

Sailor Jim and the World's Most Fantastic Hobo Shack

The silverhaired gentleman who rapped on the back door announced to my mother that he was, without a doubt, the champion kindling chopper west of the Rockies. Had he said, "Your money or your life," there was no guarantee that I would have paid attention. But the word *champion*—that did it. He had gained a second shadow.

He wore a pea jacket re-stitched at the seams with thread of various colors and a small blue cap with flat brass buttons. He took off the heavy jacket and rolled up his shirtsleeves. Good thing. It was ninety degrees in the shade of our woodshed.

I set out to pick his brain.

"Do you chop kindling for a living?"

He puffed out his round, ruddy cheeks and laughed. "I'm a sailor, lad! The captain of a proud merchantman in my day."

"But you told my mother—"

"That I was a fair hand with an ax? I'm that, all right, and many things besides."

"That you were a *champion*."

"And who's to say I'm not?" He pried the ax from the chopping block. "Ah, but I may have stretched the truth a bit. Sailors have been known to do that."

As he worked, I drank in stories of sleek clipper ships and exotic ports, waves as towering as the fir trees in the woods behind my house, storms around Cape Horn that tore out the rigging and snapped masts like toothpicks, beauty beyond words when white sails billowed like clouds in a deep-blue sky. He left with a fine meal in his stomach and his new shadow trailing at a safe distance.

My own second shadow, a black and white mutt, trailed me at an equally safe distance. I couldn't roam without him. "Go home, Stubby!" meant stay back farther than a stone's throw.

This time I didn't shout or throw stones. Soon Stubby trotted at my heels, wagging his peculiar corkscrew tail.

He knew where we were headed, even if he didn't know why. We'd ranged west through woods and fields, east to Lake Grove Park for swimming, south to the Tualatin River for fishing. North meant one place, the swamp beside the railroad tracks, Stubby's favorite playground, and mine. We once spent all day capturing and recapturing waterdogs until, toward evening, we'd gathered a hundred or more.

Sailor Jim followed the curve of the SP&S tracks toward where the low cliff beyond the swamp graded to a wooded slope. I'd never ventured close before, because of a warning.

Shortly after moving to the house on Pilkington Road, on my first trip to the swamp, I found a steam engine stopped at the water tower. The engineer invited me aboard.

"Want to take the throttle down to Remsen's Crossing?" He plopped his striped cap down over my ears, tied his red bandana around my neck, and motioned me onto his perch.

The thrill of that mile where I gripped the long handle and made the train move was dampened by dark advice: "See the smoke trailing out of those woods? That's a hobo jungle. Watch your step. If one of them grabs you, that's goodbye."

Lots of hobos had come to our house for odd jobs and meals. They didn't pose a threat. But the jungle was another matter. Still, if Sailor Jim camped there, Stubby and I could at least sneak up and peek in. That was our plan, and all we'd have done if Stubby's keen nose hadn't detected a pheasant.

Two hobos had sighted the bird and were stalking it with slingshot and gunnysack. Stubby dashed between them. The pheasant took off squawking and flapping. The hobos were furious. A rough hand grabbed the back of my neck. I was obliged to stand up straight.

"Do you know what you and that dog just did?" the man with the rough hand demanded.

I knew, but I was too scared to speak.

"Hey Boxcar," a voice called, "that's a mighty funny bird you just caught!" Laughter followed. "Looks kinda scrawny from here," another voice called. "Might get one good meal out of it, but how you ever gonna squeeze it into the pot?"

The hand relaxed and the man laughed with the others. I wasn't able to join in, seeing myself being stuffed into a pot and cooked. Then I saw Sailor Jim's twinkling eyes.

"Well lad, what brings you here? Wait, don't tell me. You caught a whiff of Boxcar's mulligan all the way from your place."

Boxcar patted my arm. "You're more than welcome. But if you'd waited five minutes we'd all be eating pheasant stew. I guess that crazy-looking mutt is welcome, too."

Panting hard, Stubby plopped down in the powdery dust beside a cardboard shack.

Shacks and lean-tos were strung up and down the slope at points where the trail zigged and zagged. A few boasted soot-blackened metal roofs and lath-and-tarpaper siding. At each campsite, Sailor Jim introduced me as "the lad who lives in the house with the board fence a mile south." Several men nodded with expressions that read, "Oh yes, that house."

The sun brushed the tree-fringed hills to the west by the time Boxcar announced first call for chow. He handed me a mound of thick, mysteriously seasoned stew on a pie tin, along with a battered soup spoon bent like a ladle. Stubby ate from a piece of cardboard turned up at the edges.

After dinner, we sat around a campfire. I listened from Sailor Jim's shadow as one hobo after another described fantastic exploits and adventures, speaking matter-of-factly in soft, low tones. I was sure I'd fallen in with Paul Bunyan, John Henry and every folk hero I'd ever read about.

The dark sky was sprinkled with stars. Mom and Dad had no idea where I was. I jumped up.

Sailor Jim chuckled. "I was beginning to wonder, lad. Thought maybe you'd decided to toss in with us."

When the folks told me to go to bed without supper, I just

grinned. Next morning, as Stubby and I skipped down the tracks, I realized I had forgotten to ask the most important question of all. I promptly did.

"How do so many 'bos know to come to my house?"

"Well now, young friend, if I told you that, it'd be like you showing someone your secret hiding place."

I promised not to breathe a word, so Sailor Jim introduced me to the private language of the vagabond, mystic symbols dealing with every situation or condition a stranger might face. Signs warning of dogs that bite, people who shoot, water that's unsafe to drink. And signs telling of good things. Two such signs were scratched on the fence in front of my house, along with a mild warning.

I was the proudest kid in the world when I walked up to my fence, found the marks I'd somehow missed, and read: "Here, this is it, a good place for a handout," and "Good food is available here, but you will have to work for it." The mild warning said Stubby's bark was worse than his bite.

For three weeks, I spent every minute of my free time with Sailor Jim, listening to his inexhaustible fund of stories while we built the world's most fantastic hobo shack, away from the jungle, in a grove of trees beside a clear pond.

At the dump off Boones Ferry Road, we found discarded sheets of construction plywood and corrugated tin, lumber, concrete blocks, used bricks, even a half-full bag of cement.

I snuck the necessary tools from home. He pounded nails as fast as I could pull them from boards and straighten them. We cut plywood to fit the frame, tacked on tarpaper, mixed mortar, and laid bricks until we ran out.

The dump gave up a door in good repair, a window frame missing only one of four panes, a fifty-gallon oil drum easily converted to a stove, veneer paneling for the interior walls and strips of worn carpeting for the plywood floor.

Sailor Jim would "winter-in" here, returning from points north in time to enjoy Christmas Eve before a crackling fire.

Until then, I would protect the place, and he would spend the rest of the winter crafting a scale model of a China clipper as my reward.

As he made ready to leave, he told me he wanted to show me an object so precious he had never so much as mentioned its existence to anyone before. Glancing about for prying eyes, he slowly drew a gold chain from his bindle.

Then it emerged, the most dazzlingly beautiful watch I ever hope to see. Solid gold, with a platinum filigree outline of a clipper ship in full sail on frothy seas, framed by an intricate compass. The face beneath the beveled crystal displayed six small dials encircling the one that told the time. I gawked, at a loss for words. His expression told me he understood, that the proper words hadn't been invented. I cried as he trudged down the tracks and around the bend.

Protecting the place was an impossible task. Once school started, I found interests other than swamp and jungle. I went every day at first, then every other day, then only one day a week. On a crisp afternoon in mid-December, I found the shack in shambles, bricks scattered, tarpaper torn, the stove bashed in with the concrete blocks we'd arranged as a base

And Sailor Jim? I never saw him again. The sad part is, I'll never know if he disappeared from the face of the earth somewhere up north, or if he returned on Christmas Eve to find his shack destroyed, and simply kept on going.

What I Heard When the Roof Caved In

I cringed as Lake Grove Grade School burned to the ground.
Its skeleton glowed red-orange in a rain
Of sparks, and when the roof gave way, a sound

Rose like the moans of tortured souls in pain,
Capped by the screech a cloud of bats might boast.
What could it be? The question sapped my brain.

Something inside the school had turned to toast,
But what? I laughed—the answer was profound—
The grand piano giving up the ghost!

When Joe Flunked His I.Q. Test

He didn't know enough to be afraid
of tests; they were no different from tying
his shoes. He feared the unknown: like dying,
going to heaven or hell, being made
to enter dark places alone. This test,
with all its ups and downs, its ins and outs,
its twists and turns, its certainties and doubts,
was pure confection compared with the rest,
a piece of cake with frosting, one to make
his mouth water, his scalp tingle, his mind
soar. So he cut it into bits and downed
it all, bite after bite, before the break
for snacks. His teacher, Miss Deaf-dumb-and-blind,
took his score to the principal, who frowned

at our Mom: "There must have been something wrong
with his form, perhaps the master showed through,"
he intoned, "and luck has been known to skew
results." "Some children know the words to a song
after the first go-round," replied Mom, quick
to point out exceptions to the rule, she
being one. They agreed to retest. He
would repeat; she had lived with his logic
since day one, and felt she'd paid her dues.
This time the school would have to deal with him
as an equal. This time, Joe, all alone,
picked up the pace a bit, driving the screws
to teacher and principal, who stood, prim
as couplets, overseeing him atone

for unspecified sins: being too smart,
or quick on the draw, or beyond their sway.
He sent his pencil flying: "Hip-hooray!"
They must have thought he'd dropped it, the dart
hitting the floor instead of the bull's-eye,
forget the target. This time through, he'd taxed
his brain's reserves. Mom's jubilation waxed,
while teacher and principal, with a sigh,
dismissing the score as somehow compromised,
sank into a slump. It wasn't Joe's forte
to stand up and be counted. The only way
you'd get him to fight was if you surprised
him at an awkward moment. He'd resort
to theatrics to deflect or allay

your suspicions. The overriding blame
was always Joe's. He'd lead a make-believe
parade of clowns with mischief up his sleeve,
or put the great Houdini's act to shame
with his escapes. His teachers saw a glint
of brilliance here and there, a random spark
kicked clear across the measureless and dark
expanse of deepest space, as steel met flint
in Joe's hearth, but nothing to prepare them
for his flair. He'd lulled them into thinking
his less-than-stellar status was his fault,
when it was theirs and the school's stratagem
to make certain, when it came to drinking
from the well of knowledge, they called a halt

when anyone went on a bender (Joe's
other middle name, besides Eugene). Rules
atrophy when exercised by fools
like these. His black marks, stacked like dominoes
in a box, rose above the rim and spilled
over. He scattered the chits in his draft,
after breaking them to bits, and he laughed,
much as he had when he'd played Hansel, thrilled
to know bread crumbs weren't used just for stuffing
turkeys, and could be strewn willy-nilly
on stage without getting him in trouble.
The principal clapped, but he was bluffing.
In his fantasy, he slapped Joe silly
till the pin-drop silence burst his bubble.

While Joe, footloose and fancy-free, skylarked,
the rest of us fell into ranks and files,
marched to the principal's drummer, our smiles
as uniform as a youth choir's, our pride barked
like a shin, stubbed like a toe, red, and black-
and-blue. We had our differences; brothers
do. But always, I saw aspects others
missed. Whimsy spilling from his haversack,
a passion for life unmatched in this age
of conformist mediocrity, lust
in its myriad forms. Joe overdid,
convinced he had a destiny, a page
in Bartlett's *Familiar Quotations*, a bust
in the Hall of Fame. He made a good bid.

When Joe Built a Radio Transmitter

With time and energy to burn, Joe took
to prowling junk stores, buying up spare parts,
chassis, turntables, tubes. Using his smarts
and following instructions in a book,
he launched KJOE. Tchaikovsky's First
Concerto flowed from his studio late
one day, but before he could celebrate
the sweet taste of success, his bubble burst.
The switchboard lit up, blinking like a string
of Christmas lights, at KEX, where Game
Five of the World Series hung on one strike.
Fans screamed their wrath. The station vowed to wring
somebody's neck, not knowing who to blame.
Meanwhile, Joe waxed effusive through the mike,

announcing Brahms, complete with program notes,
the way a baseball commentator fills
the dead space with a player's batting skills—
in Joe's case, how the Fourth Symphony "floats
like a dark cloud over a frozen land,"
the words imprinted on the cardboard box.
Between the records and his little talks,
he kept the air waves filled. The narrow band
where baseball history was being made
was his, all his. The folks were at the store,
and I was outside, lounging on the fence,
when up the road I spied a motorcade,
two black sedans and a truck from a war
movie, with slits for windows, an immense

antenna spinning slowly overhead,
and a speaker with four horns. Fuzzy fears
crept up my spine and buzzed about my ears.
I saw the end, my body lying dead,
crisp as a strip of bacon in the beams
of Martian ray guns. Suddenly the truck
slowed to a crawl, its grid antenna stuck
in a narrowing arc. In all my dreams
I never thought my house would host a crime,
but sure enough, the truck pulled up in front
and stopped, its fixed antenna pointed straight
at me. Two men in snap-brimmed hats, meantime,
stepped from a car. The one who spoke was blunt:
"We're F.B.I. We're coming through the gate."

I ran inside and hollered up the stairs,
"They're here to take away your radio!"
Imagine their dismay when out strolled Joe,
a grin across his freckled face. Two pairs
of snap-brimmed hats popped from the second car,
six men, all told, in double-breasted suits
with shoulder-holstered gats. "You in cahoots
with anyone?" the spokesman asked. "Bizarre,"
said Joe. "It must have been the Viennese
waltzes." The folks got home before the feds
had time to rush the porch and break the door
down. With Joe's clandestine transmitter seized,
they piled back in their cars, shaking their heads
and muttering about the final score.

When Joe Drew Russia as a Class Assignment

The rules were simple enough—draw the name
of a country from the box, get a book,
look up the facts, write them down. Joe mistook
a simple paper for a path to fame.
He'd learn the works—what makes the Russians tick,
what Russians think of this and that, how they
approach their lives and jobs, and how they play.
His stabs at research ran into one brick
wall after another. Russia was *Red,*
he was told at the library. The word
seemed to strike fear, as if the color burned
the throats and lips of those poor souls who said
Red right out loud. But Joe was undeterred.
The more they told him no, the more he yearned

to learn, so he typed a letter and stuck
it in a business envelope addressed
to the Russian Ambassador. The rest
was easy—lick the stamp and trust to luck.
Next on his list, he went downtown and bought
a current copy of *Soviet Life*
at Rich's Cigar Store. With his jackknife,
he cut out the subscription form and shot
it off. Then he penned a personal note
to Joseph Stalin, asking him to ship
a loaf of Russian bread, and enough cheese
to share with his class, and perhaps a quote
he could use in his paper—a wry quip.
As an afterthought, he wrote: "P.S. *Please!*"

The magazine arrived, his first return!
Next, the Soviet Ambassador's third
secretary wrote to say he'd assured
Joe a stack of brochures, so he could learn
how great their system is, vis-à-vis ours,
which he characterized as decadent
and imperialistic. "Excellent!"
said Joe, who read the way a bear devours
a pot of honey, not missing a lick.
With Russians nibbling at his line, he fished
as one familiar with a hook, but caught
more than he bargained for. It made me sick
to see the black sedans again. I wished
myself aloft, but my pinions were shot.

Down Pilkington Road they crept, at a pace
designed to plant seeds of doubt in a strong-
willed mind. I wondered, what have I done wrong
this time? Did Old Man Janik plead his case
before a judge, since he thinks he controls
the swamp, Southern Pacific right-of-way
and all, where Stubby and I like to play,
and chases us on his frequent patrols,
armed with a shotgun full of rock salt? That
fantasy was dashed when the Buicks braked
in front of our white board fence, and a head
poked from a rolled-down window, snap-brimmed hat
and all, and called: "This here *Joe's* house?" I faked
nonchalance, though I saw Joe lying dead,

riddled with bullets from their tommy guns,
while they stood around and joked, cigarettes
dangling from their loose lower lips, placing bets
on who pumped in the most lead slugs, like Huns
at a barbarian turkey shoot. "Yes,"
I said, not wanting to suffer a fate
worse than death at their hands. "If you'll just wait—"
They sprang from their cars like jackals. My guess
was, they viewed me as the lookout, and Joe
would take it on the lam if I tipped him
off. Joe wandered out and a G-man moaned.
"It's him again," he bawled, "the radio
whiz kid." The situation went from grim
to comical, the way six grown men groaned

and shuffled their feet. I wanted to ask
what Joe had done this time to pull them from
their more important chores, and why so glum,
but my vocal chords weren't up to the task,
having swallowed a laugh. The spokesman spoke
with a Southern drawl: "Yo' daddy at home?"
"Nyet," said Joe. The men swayed like metronome
wands, set to grab their gats. "If that's a joke—"
said the spokesman. But before they could haul
Joe off to prison, shackled hand and foot,
the folks drove up, and with a reprimand,
the G-men left, muttering about all
the Commie pinkos they had hoped to put
away that day, and all the contraband.

Four:

The Rose to Saint Louis

The Rose to Saint Louis

Aboard the Portland Rose, June 1, 1948

The Sandy River hops, skips and jumps across
the choppy face of the Columbia, rampaging
halfway to the Washington shore in the flood
the *Oregon Journal* calls the worst since 1894.
I bound across the aisle for a better look
and watch white water jam the piers of the old
railroad bridge with tree trunks and branches,

matted grass from washed-out banks, painted
boards, and odd debris. The engineer stops,
throws the Rose in reverse, and backs down
the tracks toward town, observation car first.
scenes roll slowly past the way a film rewinds,
until at last we pass, down in Sullivan's Gulch,
the tree where I swung, on Mackie's double-dare,

one-handed through smoke raging from the Rose,
like a knight in a fire-breathing dragon's lair.
We switch at last to the north-south tracks
and clickety-clack through the old Albina Yard,
scene of many a bold adventure. Like the time
Mackie got the hot-shot notion to roll tires
from the dump on the bluff down on a cluster

of cinderdicks warming their hands by a fire
in a rusted-out oil drum, waiting for a freight,
its brakes hissing, its stack belching thick smoke,
its wheels screeching the tracks like fingernails
across a blackboard, to pull to a stop. The bulls
dodged bouncing tires, hurling fists at the bluff,
while hoboes, hopping from the open boxcars,

scattered like flies. Or the time Mackie told
the green kid he'd give him a silver dollar just
for jumping off the bluff, and the fish swallowed
Mackie's line clear to the sinker, the part about
how the cartwheel was down there in a pair of old
pants among the tin cans, inner tubes and busted
bottles strewn at the base of the talus slope.

The hick jumped, then struggled back up through
blackberry vines choking a cut in the steep bank,
crying his eyes out, and nursing scraped elbows
and assorted welts. And, clutching a pair of wool
trousers. Mackie turned the one bulging pocket
inside out and spilled the contents in a heap.
Fifty-two moldy one dollar Silver Certificates,

a 20-dollar gold piece, a Liberty Head half, six
Standing Liberty quarters, five Buffalo nickels,
nine Indian Head pennies, and a Morgan cartwheel!
The kid, happy as a dumb clam, snatched his loot
and ran. Mackie and I divvied up. He took all
the paper, and I got the coins for my collection,
except for the gold piece, which my parents gave

to the police. Mackie and I went back, and time
after time, left with nothing but cuts from busted
glass, and bruises from falls. Old pufferbellies,
some steamed up for switching, others stone cold,
point from the roundhouse like spokes from a hub.
Water laps at the seawall lip as we creep past
the ghost of Henry Kaiser's Swan Island Shipyard,

where the rusted ribs of abandoned Victory ships
frame cranes curved like question marks. In 1943,
my first grade classmates at Alameda School and I

helped a five-star admiral and the Governor's wife,
shy behind the veil polka-dotting her face, boldly
launch a giant bottle at a light aircraft carrier,
the U.S.S. Bunker Hill, until, on the fourth try,

it broke, showering champagne on teachers leaning
beneath the scaffold for a closer look, while we,
laughing to tears, stood on our toes and clapped.
The war still seems real: The air raid drills,
monitors pulling down tall shades with long poles
while everybody cringed beneath the nearest desk,
fearing the first bomb's burst, War Bond stamps

bought with nickels and dimes clutched in sweaty
fists, saving fat in canning jars, taking scrap
metal to the Hollywood Theatre for free admission
to the Saturday matinee, and on that sunny day
when daffodils packed the boxes along the porch
and tulips lined the walk, and the air was filled
with talk about how, any day now, the war would

wind to a halt and the boys would all come home,
the telegram regretting to inform me that my Uncle
Hank, whose laugh I hear, whose grin I see as he
pulls his disappearing dime from my ear, is dead.
What the photo spread in yesterday's *Journal* failed
to show is that nothing remains of Oregon's second
largest city. Vanport is gone. Dad said "No, no,"

over and over on the phone with Elmore Roecker,
who was standing on the Slough Bridge when the dike
broke and the whole works was picked up and swept
toward Astoria, two-story buildings bobbing like
corks in the flotilla of wartime shipyard workers'
houses, though few lives were lost, the paper said,
because nobody paid attention when the engineers

proclaimed the dike as sound as the dollar, urged
folks to return to their homes, and packed their
instruments away. Somehow the railroad trestle
held, though as we inch across I feel it sway
above the silent movie waves shaking fists
at the pale sky. Nana takes my hand and tells me,
over and over, there's not a thing to worry about,

just as she did the time when I was five, sitting
at the wheel of her Oldsmobile sedan, pretending I
was a racecar driver rounding turns on two wheels,
and a drunk grabbed his Broadway cabbie by the neck,
crashing the taxi smack into Nana's trunk. Questions
thrown by the police careened through my empty head,
bouncing off the hollow walls. Nana, clear-eyed,

declared both car and me fit for a visit to the zoo.
We make it across to the Washington side and switch
to the east-west tracks. It seems strange to see
Vancouver, Camas and Washougal pass as islands off
our port beam, and green-and-yellow turtles swim
circles in starboard shallows clear above the rails.
It's not the way I'd fantasized at all: The Rose

charging beneath steep basalt walls rising like
jagged teeth gouging the Earth, and me between cars,
tasting the air where spray from waterfalls drifts
across the tracks, waterfalls named by storytellers
for ancient events, the time Multnomah's daughter,
when told to turn her back on love, jumped instead,
turning to tears, and christened afresh by pioneers

who took one look and called them Horsetail, Bridal
Veil and Mist, since waterfalls in the wilderness
clearly had no names, and that's how they appeared.

Now my trusty geology book, the one my Uncle Hank
bought me after he saw my rock collection and heard
the whole tale of how old Doc Adams had drilled
appreciation into what he called my chock-a-block

brain, or bonehead, depending, fills in details
of landslides and lava flows I missed on all those
Sunday drives up the Gorge, blinded by fights over
who got to sit in the front seat of our '34 Plymouth
and play with the radio knobs as a way to rub salt
in his brothers' wounds. When old Doc Adams caught
Gene Wonderlick and me with claw hammers, chipping

chunks of crystal geodes, opal and agatized wood
from the monumental rock garden rising to meet his
Mason Street home, he gave us a choice: We could
face the music before our parents and the "proper
authorities," or show up every Saturday at the crack
of dawn, corrected to eight o'clock sharp, to learn
all about our glittering booty, the bright stones

and 30-million-year-old clams he sent home with us
as reminders. Weighing the alternatives had taken
two seconds. Doc Adams walked me through the ages,
pausing everywhere to hand me pieces of the past.
He taught me to use my senses, to pick up the sweet
smell inside glass cabinets where fossils breathe
their own air, the tart taste of alum, the optical

illusion of seeing double through a calcite rhomb,
the rough brush of pumice, the soft stroke of talc,
and the colors! A columnar basalt formation looms,
rounded at the top like a mushroom cap. Beacon Rock.
Over in Oregon, Multnomah's daughter weeps buckets.
Oneonta Gorge seems a thin line at this distance,
that mysterious cleft Dad led us into, clutching

shoes and socks, our pant legs rolled up, skipping
across sharp rocks, slipping on slimy streamers
and smooth stones in the shallow creek, and laughing
when younger brother Cappy sat kersplash in a pool,
and older brother Joe stepped in a hole disguised
as a boulder, and I dropped to my knees like a shot
with a sticker stuck in the ball of my foot, all

laughing but the one immersed in the current mess,
until at last we stood at the base of Oneonta Falls
as in a great cathedral, bathed in shimmering mist,
craning our necks and shading our eyes to drink in
light, dazzling through emerald ferns and malachite
moss, as the noontide sun swept across the narrow
arc of sky, high overhead. Bonneville Dam, as if

to gauge our progress, brings with it the first call
for supper. We're half an hour from home, but more
than five hours on the train, cowcatcher plowing water.
The wand dances up and down the small-scale xylophone.
The tall black man in the starched white jacket grins
like the timpanist in the opera orchestra the time
my fourth grade class listened to songs from Carmen

for three weeks, and I was thrilled to find I could
follow everything. Nana and I take the first table
on the river side. "Port out, starboard home," she
informs me with her air of mystery. Light slanting
through windows from the west magnifies the depth
of lacquer layered on the bright mahogany woodwork.
When I hold my napkin ring up close, I see the face

reflected in the Fun House mirror at Jantzen Beach.
The Bridge of the Gods passes as if we're the ones
standing still while it swings on its axis to let

the ghosts of tall ships slip past. Its silver
girders, anchored to remnants of the ancient land
bridge, trigger a myth: Wy'east and Pahto battled
here, hurling fireballs and thunderbolts to win

the love of Loo-wit, until one day Coyote, tiring
of all the to-do, tromped on the bridge and went
away wiping his hands, leaving Wy'east and Pahto
out in the cold, collecting snow, waiting to be
reduced to mountains and named for mortal men,
Wy'east for Viscount Admiral Hood, who never even
came to see it, and Pahto for President John Adams,

reflecting somebody's bright idea to take the peaks
of the Cascades, and like the up-and-down streets
of Oregon City, make them monuments to Great White
Chiefs, changing the works to The Presidents' Range.
Loo-wit, her perfect cinder cone the spitting image
of Japan's Fujiyama, now named Mount Saint Helens
for a British sloop, slept through the whole thing.

I order chicken à la king, delighting in the fact
that it's served up steaming from under a silver
dome, and topped by melted cheese poured
from a silver gravy boat. And the clickety-clack
Is like music, the side to side sway like a dance,
when Nana and I at last adjust to our upper berth,
hush our goodnights, turn out the light, and race

through the blackness, faster than a speeding
bullet. In the morning, we pass a water tower
in the town where Nana, a brand new teacher, met
Mister Parsons, the dashing young man who parts
his hair in the middle and smiles from the small
oval frame on my mother's vanity, the father she
never knew, who looks to me like a true lover

of life. Mom looks a lot like him when her eyes
gaze to infinity, and she holds her head just so,
the shape of her nose, her lips stretched as if
the smile behind is poised to spring, the way his
is in the faded photo she takes to the sun room
sometimes, and talks to. I asked her to watch
corn hills where I, breaking scientific ground,

planted three yellow perch in a circle of seven
seeds in every mound, peat moss worked to where
the dirt crumbled deep beneath, and to please
pour on the water, pull weeds, cut the grass down
and string tinfoil strips to keep the crows away,
"And yes, I promise to write, and I love you, too!"
My eyes snap wide open as a deep voice chuckles,

"Would you like your water glass refilled, young
man?" The white letters on the waiter's black
nameplate, close enough to touch, introduce him
as Louis. "No relation to the saint!" he laughs,
lifting my glass and pouring ice water as if by
magic, across a vast expanse of space, spilling
not a drop. Nana lets the world know she frowns

on sweets by waving away my dessert as well as hers,
pudding plump with bits of fruit candy. She opens
her black leather change purse with the fancy silver
clasp, and counts out the nickels and dimes saved
for just such an occasion, lunch in the dining car.
She rises and turns. I slide slowly from my chair.
She's ten steps ahead before my feet touch the floor.

Louis winks and says to drop back in another hour,
after the last of the diners leaves, and he will
show me "over here," the "other side" of the train.

I spend the hour counting cows, beaver dams, deer,
anything to pass time, and wondering how on Earth
someone gets to the "other" side when all I see,
port and starboard, are miles of brush and scrub

trees dotting outcroppings of feldspar and schist.
Louis greets me with a wide grin. "Figured I'd be
seein' you," he says over his shoulder as he leads me
past the partition at the far end of the dining car.
"Figured you'd be needin' somethin' sweet to round out
the peas and mashed potatoes." The kitchen comes
to a standstill, all eyes fixed on me, not a smile

on a single face, as if we'd caught them at the game
where everybody freezes on command. The skinny kid
with the Brooklyn Dodgers cap turned clear around
hangs above the deep metal sink, up to his elbows
in suds. The gray-haired man with the raised scar
down his cheek holds pans of dough for dinner rolls
poised at the oven door. The man with the square

hat folded from *Smokey Stover* in the Sunday funnies,
arms bulging from a sleeveless tee shirt, stands
with only the tip of his wedge-shaped knife touched
to the chopping block, the blade halfway through
a bundle of celery stalks. I'd never even given it
a thought, but not one Negro lives in Lake Grove,
or Oswego, or Tualatin, although a lot of them come

to fish beside the railroad tracks where they can,
like along Lakewood Bay, a stone's throw from State
Street, where whole families spend the day, casting
their lines from the jerry-built steps left behind
when the Chinese gandy dancers living in the little
yellow houses with the fake-brick tarpaper roofs
vanished without a trace. I'd shake my head when

gandy dancers paid me a princely fifty cents apiece
for carp in the two- to four-foot range. I knew
where to find and how to catch them: The Duck Pond
with a ball of white bread on a Number Six hook.
I'd haul them the mile and a half to Lakewood Bay,
hands bloody from the sharp gills, as many as I could
at a time, making seven dollars on a good day,

better than two crummy 18-hole double-bag rounds
at one of the country clubs, breaking my back
and rubbing my shoulders raw. But a carp?
A slimy, scaly, bony, bottom-feeding whitefish
that thrives on frogs, ducklings, and scum?
I'd say the worst things I could think of, like
"This fish here is full of duck droppings!" and

"This fine specimen ate nothing but frog barf!"
And they would grin and nod their heads, and look
at one another, discussing each fish as if it were
a relative fresh off the boat, and making me feel
that fifty cents apiece was a heck of a deal. My hands
seem strangely pale and out of place when I catch
A glimpse. I casually stuff them in my pockets.

Louis introduces me around and tells me each man's
title. I forget how white I look and shake with
Chef and Fourth Cook alike, and everybody lets off
a little steam, whooping and hollering, while I,
relieved, smile. Louis scoops out two mounds
of peppermint-stripe ice cream, and sits with me
at the Chef's end, on round chairs that fold down

from the wall at the only window open to the wind.
Wrapping the breeze around my face, I work up
courage enough to ask: "How do they move about

in such tight quarters?" Louis flings his arms wide
and bellows, "They go with the flow!" I see what
he means as they pirouette and mime like acrobats,
and trip the light fantastic when the smoke clears.

Louis points out just what a great land America is,
seen from a train: The farms with windmill towers
and plain white houses, the small towns whose church
steeples rise like Gothic spires, the grain elevators,
rivers and bridges, hills and valleys, the red-tailed
hawk on the weathered fence post, the barefoot kid
raising a bamboo pole in one hand, a string of brook

trout in the other, signs placed at the sides of roads by
the Burma Shave people and the puzzling Technocrats,
hobo jungles whose campfires sew white asbestos threads
in the azurite sky, safe havens where the homeless rest
along the way. "We're all brothers and we're only
passin' through," says Louis, waving back at a weary
face floating in a green thicket bordering a stream.

St. Louis is a blur. Uncle Fred materializes like
a boiled potato from the engine's belch and hiss, his
belly button bulging like a cartoon eyeball inside
a white tee shirt wet at the armpits. Aunt Lorraine
and Cousin Donna pop from Uncle Fred's sides like
Laurel and Hardy waving invisible derbies. More like
Laurel and Laurel, since they can stand side by side

behind him and not be noticed. I get a wet kiss
on one cheek, and the sound of one on the other.
Cousin Donna is thinner than any person I ever saw,
standing sideways in her eighth grade graduation
portrait, wearing a formal with yards of frills
to "fill out what nature forgot," Aunt Lorraine
tells Nana, nudging her with an elbow and winking.

Donna plays *Bye Bye Blackbird* on her ukulele,
and all the kids in her neighborhood sing along,
and gradually I learn the words, though they don't
make much sense. And we all chase after fireflies
and fall beneath their spell, in the heat where
everybody drips and the sheets soak through in no
time. And all we talk about in the morning is how

not one of us could sleep a wink, and what's more,
a scorcher's in store. We sit for hours, fanning
ourselves over iced tea with mint leaves picked
from the herb garden outside the kitchen window,
doing what Nana calls "catching up," and Lorraine
calls "gossipin'," and Donna calls "horsefeathers,"
and Fred calls "claptrap," though he gets his licks

in, every chance he can, and doesn't miss a trick
when it comes to one-upmanship. I call it lively
entertainment, as if I'm watching total strangers
act out scenes from a play. The best part is, it's
real, and they're my relatives. It's a scorcher,
all right. Fred is beet-red when he bursts Nana's
balloon in mid-sentence by shouting he's "gassed

up the jalopy," and I give him thumbs-up through
the screen door. I never knew of a zoo so grand!
And the show they put on! The elephants take tiny
steps to avoid the heels just ahead as they parade
in their Betty Boop sailor suits, standing up with
one front foot on the next back, the other waving.
Poodles in pink tutus ride motorcycles in circles.

Chihuahuas in sombreros and serapes, or flowered
skirts and peasant blouses, dance to the folk tune
we played and sang in our sixth grade class musical,

where I, being in the chorus, could afford to forget
a line or two. I carry tons of such memories around.
Everything reminds me of something, and right on cue,
the play makes me think of the time Mary Lou and Lois

took me aside and told me my fly was wide open, then
stood their ground and looked away while I, my face
red as a Christmas bulb, pulled up my zipper and fled.
It took three tries, over a week's time, to make eye
contact with either one, and each time we did, over
the next several weeks, I blushed. Nana buys me
a snow cone, telling the girl three times before

the words sink in, to "please leave off the syrup."
Uncle Fred says the ape is going crazy, leaping about
from bar to knotted rope to tire swing and back to bar.
I hug the ground and squeeze my way between stiletto
heels and seersucker cuffs, trying to get up front
where I can see what's really going on, why people
jump back on the left and press ahead on the right,

then switch like clockwork, and why rainbows spatter
silk stockings, and tiny atom bombs explode as dust
bursts on black patent leather shoes and two-toned
oxfords. I reach the open circle where people dance
and laugh hysterically in time to watch the ape's
loose lips curl back, and a monumental blob of water
sail forth and miss, by an inch, the blue-and-white

striped dress in my line of sight, hitting me splat.
People tell me how I "walked into one that time," and
I try laughing as an alternative to turning red, and
it works. Turning red, after all, is for kids, and
I'm going on twelve. I've traveled to St. Louis, and
dined on grilled sole across the Great Divide, and
taken in the world's most famous zoo, and learned

what a great land we live in, with its red-tailed
hawks, and its Technocracy signs, and Louis, who is,
in my mind, a saint. The Rose went back home after
dropping Nana and me in St. Louis. On the Vista Dome
Streamliner whisking us through the night to St. Paul,
filled with the moon's light, I see corn ten feet tall,
with ears as long as baseball bats and fat as blimps.

Shoot-out at the Main Street Five & Dime

Six days a week, Dad drove across Rosemont Road from our home in Lake Grove to his store in Oregon City, Hedges 5-10-25, known as the Main Street Five & Dime.

Every evening, he painted vivid word pictures of sunrises, sunsets, freshly plowed fields, wildflowers, deer, tall grass billowing in the breeze, snow on the Cascades in a sweep from Mt. Rainier to Mt. Jefferson, always something new.

I rode with him on Saturdays and worked as a stock boy. My first task was to wipe nose prints off the front door glass where little kids stared wide-eyed at the long candy case, its narrow glass-fronted bins displaying everything from lemon drops to chocolate creams, before stepping inside, pennies clutched in sweaty fists, to buy their treats.

Next up, I tended to the turtles, goldfish, and parakeets, swept the aisles clean with a wide dust mop, and stocked shelves from bins in the cramped confines of the basement.

One day I investigated the dark spaces beneath the bins. Dim shapes lurked at the back of one. I squeezed in as far as I could. Slowly, using a long oil measuring stick, I rolled a small object toward the aisle—a pestle pecked out of gray basalt! Then came two perfectly round gray basalt mortars, then two more pestles, one broken, an enormous rolling pin pestle, and a stunning hammerhead grooved in the middle!

I dragged Dad downstairs. He said we had to inform the landlord, since the objects were rightfully his. The landlord said they came from the excavation for the Oregon City Post Office, on the bluff just downstream from Willamette Falls. He picked up the mortars, said he would use them as doorstops.

I bristled. "You can't do that! These are priceless artifacts! They belong in the Clackamas County Historical Museum!"

Looking through me like I didn't exist, he walked off with his doorstops. Smiling down at the hammerhead and assorted pestles, I knew someday I would give them to the museum.

When Joe Fell Out of the Tree

Seventy-five feet is a long way down
when you're clinging to limbs, as I was when
Joe shot past, squawking like a barnyard hen
on a chopping block, waving like a crown
prince at a coronation. He climbed trees
the way some kids pick off your prized cat's-eyes
with peewees, or do swan dives, or swat flies
over the left field fence, or take to skis—
he blazed his own trails. The machine-gun *crack-*
crack as branch after branch spit toothpicks
shattered what remained of my brain. I thought
I was dead, parachute lines tangled, ack-
ack fire bursting like popcorn. "Fiddlesticks!"
yelled Joe, who, for all his falling, was not

what you'd call overwrought. I stole a glance,
expecting Humpty-Dumpty's broken shell,
or the scattered remnants of Little Nell,
her hero delayed by a game of chance,
knowing the railroad never runs on time,
but there was Joe, up and moving with ease,
though turning in tight circles, a trapeze
artist taking a bow, a pantomime
maestro mimicking a marionette
in the ballet from *The Nutcracker Suite.*
It took Dad three tedious hours to talk
me to the ground, telling me to forget
where I was, and feel my way with my feet.
I'd stick my fingers in some pitch, and balk,

or hear Joe crashing past again, and freeze,
or catch a whiff of green fir, and replay
the sharp rain of needles, the ricochet
of twigs and splinters, the way the tree's
trunk swayed, creaking like a ship's timbered hull
in a typhoon, through the ear I kept pressed
to the bark, listening, as one possessed,
for signs of my imminent doom. As skull-
and-crossbones billowed off the quarterdeck,
Dad snatched me from the jaws of death,
telling me Mom had gone with Joe, we'd hear
what the Doc had to say: "No broken neck
or ribs or other bones, no shortened breath
or dizziness, no cause to raise a fear,

yet X-rays show a fracture in his leg
when he was five or so, and it was never set,
though it seems to have healed well." What you get
when you live with a kid who has no peg
to perch himself upon, no pirate's hook
to plant in anybody's bounty, no
mind to undertows at work in the flow
of tides, are tales enough to fill a book.
He returned home in no time, his whole
outlook as upbeat as can be, and spoke
in glowing terms of his hospital stay,
the night-time nurse whose ministrations stole
his heart, the á la carte menu a joke,
the countless opportunities to play.

The Model Boat Contest

The Strouds are Canadian, from Ontario, where folks say *oot* and *aboot* instead of out and about. They're short, five-four or so. Old Man Stroud wraps his salt-and-pepper hair around the back of his bald head like a horseshoe. She sweeps hers up and holds it there with the longest bobby pins I ever saw.

Retired, they buy the vacant grocery store where Lower Drive intersects Pilkington Road. Of all the stores in all the out-of-the-way locations, they pick the one a quarter-mile from my home!

They keep the furnishings, sweep the wood floor daily before laying down fresh sawdust.

I hang around the store because I like the way it smells, and because Old Man Stroud is a grump with a grin. I laugh at the way he tells stories, all by-gosh-and-by-golly, with brimming eyes and rosy cheeks. When I offer to do odd jobs, he barks that he's the only yokel qualified to do odd jobs.

Mrs. Stroud, no disrespect to Mom, is someone I might adopt if the need arises. She keeps the produce thinned and sprinkled, makes sure the meat smells good, gives me free licorice twists. I buy candy bars and Popsicles to keep suspicions down, so she doesn't think I'm a mooch.

In mid-June, Old Man Stroud announces a contest open only to grade school kids in the immediate area. An unspecified prize awaits the one who crafts the best model boat. I see myself in the limelight, though model boat building is brand new to me.

I want to know every type of boat there is. I settle on a sloop and look it up: "A single-masted sailing boat rigged fore-and-aft with a headsail extending from the foremast to the bowsprit."

Cool! I have until the Fourth of July to carve and shape and sand the sleekest sloop afloat. I measure, draw to proportion, and assemble materials and tools.

I imagine a spindrift sea, my soon-to-be creation splitting crests, plowing troughs in a race dubbed once-in-a-lifetime, with critics hailing my sloop's revolutionary design. I screw weights on the keel and splash like mad in the bathtub on the trial run, to make sure she's seaworthy and won't capsize.

I improvise some elements of superstructure, such as how to attach a mast. Sewing sails is a snap. The rigging is simplified from what I see in pictures.

I paint her white, three coats, sanded in between. In honor of our nation's founding, I christen her *Miss Liberty*.

A sparse crowd assembles at Stroud's Grocery at noon on the Fourth. Old Man Stroud holds out the only two entries turned in, mine and that of an on-and-off friend from across the street, who smirks when I say let the best man win. I owe him one.

His boat doesn't fit any type I found in my hours of research. Essentially it's a four-by-six piece of half-inch plywood sawed to a point at one end. A smaller piece is attached to that, and an even smaller piece is nailed on top. People politely clap when Old Man Stroud says "Second Place."

That makes me "First!" I don't care first of what, the thrill of knowing I've won, even when only two are in the race, opens vast possibilities.

The prize, a copper horse, will shine in my eyes forever—as will the glow on Old Man Stroud's face as he holds my boat high, eyes filled to spilling.

The Barnum & Bailey Train

Boones Ferry Crossing, 1949

I roll the morning papers
one by one, stuff my bags tight,
ride my bike head and shoulders above
thick fog hunkered in the hollow,
strain against the steep hill
hovering beyond the tracks.
In a blink, the Barnum & Bailey train
appears. Cars with molded curlicues
of gold and ruby, silver and jade,
hug the cotton plane like candy-
sprinkled cookies floating in a bowl
of milk. I brake at the crossing sign,
hold my breath, stand as still as I can.
The engine stops at the water tower;
steam swirls about the wheels
like drifting snow. The calliope
sounds a string of shrill notes. Roustabouts
bob in the fog like shipwreck victims,
pitching hay, filling water troughs
from wooden buckets, ribbed undershirts,
felt hats, suspenders, the uniform of the day.
Baffled windows squint in the pearly light:
elephant trunk, lion head, tiger tail,
flashes of pale flesh, brocades and bright
feathers. Agog, I peek inside a universe
reserved for those with passes, today's news
already old, cold, forgotten in fog.

The Eternal Years Are Hers

It wasn't that she looked twice
in my shy direction, though I knew
she did, and she knew I looked back
through air fogged by my obvious breath,
there at the school bus stop as she
swung books behind, off down the hill,
or that a kid I knew said she did
things I could only vaguely conjure,
there in the heat beneath thick winter
blankets, hand on my new manhood;

it wasn't that I saw up her skirt
on the tree house ladder that sultry
afternoon, past heels the pink
of plum blossoms, aglow like rose
quartz pebbles turned round
in a mountain stream, past tanned calves
golden downed as no one I knew
had told me they could be,
past backs of knees, thighs that parted
like parentheses as she took steps
with motions I could only vaguely trace
through senses dulled by pounding eyes;

it wasn't that she wore no underpants
beneath her light print skirt,
or that later, in my room at home,
when she pulled on a pair of my jeans
and slipped her skirt high over her head,
her cotton sweater rose in slow motion,
and she wore no bra, and her breasts shone
with a glow I could only vaguely re-create,
there in the heat between thin summer sheets;

it wasn't that we touched fingertips
on the path to the tent in the woods
behind my house, brushing aside the low
limbs, our thighs parting the ripe grass,
the hair on my tanned arms standing
straight out in the charged air, her laughter
flashing at the spark, the sun soft
through fir boughs, the tent hot, its olive
weave alive with effervescent stars
above the wood and canvas cot, or that
she smelled of wheat straw and honey;

it was that my jug-eared little brother
squealed, then danced at Dad's heels,
hollering about how he'd seen me
sneak inside the tent, and how I had
a girl with me, and how I was bound
to be in trouble now, that bends me
to her will in dreams, a slave to the way
she places kisses on my face, her soft
lips fluttering like butterfly wings,
her fingertips, light as breezes,
tingling my thighs as the tent falls,
and I, like the walls of Jericho,
come tumbling down.

When Joe Upset the Applecart
at the Oswego Lake Canal

My first mistake was telling Joe a gang
of guys from my class planned to skinny-dip
at the wide spot where barges used to slip
past each other in the old days, and hang
out on the flats among the scrub oaks and flood-
borne boulders, working on our tans. I made
it sound so good he signed aboard. I prayed
he'd mind his Ps and Qs, owing to blood
being thicker than water. He'd pulled tricks
on me before. It was a chalk-dry day,
and the Canal a first-rate place to be,
where echoes of sledgehammers and steel picks
resonate with ghostly tones when you lay
your ear against bedrock, topography

stripped of its mantle, basalt in the raw,
just as it cooled in a Miocene sea—
but that was me, seeing geology
everywhere. This is about what Joe saw
that nobody else got to. I ran stark
naked through the scrub brush, jumped like a fool
and swung from the rope, out over the pool,
but as I let go and splashed to the dark
depths, I spied, a mile down the leaf-bright dale,
three females from our class. Breathless, emerging
from the water, I signaled with my hands,
Stay calm, three girls are coming up the trail,
keep out of sight! I zeroed in, urging
Joe to hold his decibels down. Brass bands

are known to follow him. The scene dissolved
to nine boys, cloistered in their private cells,
watching three girls pop from their cotton shells
like butterflies. My stunned senses revolved
around red toenails blazing like stop lights,
pedal pushers taking hours to slip past
the first knees and hours more to clear the last
ankles, peasant blouses soaring to heights
and floating overhead like parachutes,
screams and giggles as the girls danced about,
each daring another to be the first
to drop her bra. One did, and "they were beauts,"
Joe told the guys he'd startled with his shout
from atop the tallest boulder. The worst

calamities of my life were those whose
wounds left scars. The time in the fifth grade
when I broke my nose after having made
the winning touchdown in the slime and ooze,
sliding face-first into the goal post. Or
when I was seven and chipped my front
teeth on a drinking fountain, a dumb stunt,
showing off. Or when I was ten, before
I could step from the punt, somebody jerked
the line and I fell back, cracking my block-
head on the motor mount. Now I was faced
with social failure. Ostracism lurked
in my classmates' eyes. The absolute shock
of the terrible loss, the utter waste!

I was torn between intense emotions—
rage for the wonderful rush, gone for good,
woe for not having fully understood
Joe's eccentricities, his larks, oceans
apart from mine. At least he'd thought to yank
his swimming trunks back on, for which I blessed
the ghost of Uncle Hank. The girls were dressed
by then. They scattered barbed remarks point-blank,
flushing the chastened hunters from their blind.
We drifted out. Their glossy contours shone
like those of dancers through their seventh veils,
a sight boys see in visions, ill-defined.
The clear reality was Joe's alone.
He had a gift. Oh, I could tell you tales.

A Day at Lake Grove Park

Lower Drive is paved with tar over gravel
so the country mile between home and park
is a trough of hot coals. I don't wear shoes,
so I stick to weeds and patches of dry grass.

After a quick dip, a few laps, I lie face down
on the dock on my terry cloth towel, listening.
Waves lap against the stilts. In the distance,
outboard motors buzz, cough, and sputter.

Kids squeal and scream as they trot past,
heel and toe, not so fast that the lifeguard
shifts her focus from improving her suntan
and blows her whistle, but just fast enough.

Flat as a flounder on a board, I feel the sun
shrink the droplets polka-dotting my back.
Through the crack, I watch silver minnows
dart in and out of colonies of leafy moss.

In the fall I start West Linn High. The rest
of the universe is lost on me. Where I live
and what I do are all I know. In my world
I swim, soak up the sun, hope and dream.

Five:
Chug-a-Lugging the Champ
at the *Arsenic and Old Lace* Cast Party

Chug-a-Lugging the Champ
at the *Arsenic and Old Lace* Cast Party

It's no surprise I played a minor role
Considering that no one else in the cast
Was under seventeen—I was the sole
Apprentice footman vying in a vast

Tableau with seasoned drama kings and queens.
My lines were few and far between, but fear
Still snuck in and struck between my scenes.
"It's party time, let's go and drink some beer!"

Al crooned. Final curtain, parties were par.
Cold cream and wads of tissue paper took
The greasepaint off. Char left her door ajar
While changing. I pretended not to look.

We all piled into cars. Our motorcade
Snaked up to Skylands, with its sweeping view
Of nighttime lights. Developers had laid
A grid of gravel roads. I never knew

A bliss to rival this. The seniors chose
A spot and made a circle of their cars.
Music from a dozen radios
Reverberated in my ears. The stars

Beamed down like thespians of all the plays
Performed on all the stages throughout time.
I never liked the taste of beer, but raise
A stubby with a bunch of peers?—sublime!

Stu, the chug-a-lug champ at West Linn High,
Went begging for contenders, his renown
Was such. I kissed my innocence goodbye
By telling everyone I'd take the crown.

The beers I'd downed had made me bold
Beyond all reason. Giggles and guffaws
Erupted when I asked Stu how to hold
The bottle and what else to do because

I'd never chug-a-lugged before. Two quarts
Appeared. I hadn't thought this far ahead.
That was a lot of beer. I'd read reports.
What if I drowned? What if I wound up dead?

"Open your throat," Stu said with a fiendish grin.
"Gravity will do the rest." *That's all?*
I thought. Al gave the signal to begin.
What happened next I really don't recall

Except, to my amazement, cast and crew
Began to whoop and cheer. I tried to laugh
But belched and farted. Then I heard poor Stu
Not only lost, I cut his time in half.

Gracious in defeat, he nonetheless
Requested a rematch. "Let's wait and see,"
I answered, saturated with success.
"I need a nap, but first I have to pee."

How Mary Lou Moved

It was one thing running naked through the woods beside
the canal with guys from my seventh grade class, crowing
like cocks, pairing in thickets and behind giant rocks
for a little diddling, gathering in the clearing after skinny-
dipping and sunning our brown bodies until somebody
got it up and we all fell laughing into a quick-draw contest.

It was another thing having Mary Lou sitting on my lap
in the back seat as somebody's dad drove five of us couples
to our first high school football game and for all my trying
I couldn't keep it down, and Mary Lou kept squirming
around laughing as we swung into curves, brushing my
hands, right and left, with her cashmere covered breasts.

Getting it up had seemed so free and easy with the guys,
and now hot lava coursed through my veins, steam
venting at the buttoned collar of my Stradivarius shirt,
layered under Lord Jeff sweater and leather-sleeved jacket,
hotter and hotter—until Mary Lou melted in a blur
of stop signs and streetlights and tilted telephone poles.

The stands were bone-chilling cold, a perfect reason
to keep my jacket snapped and my hands in my pockets.
The game whizzed by, and when my parents asked
who won and I said "I did" they passed it off laughing
and said "Goodnight" and I said "Right," thinking about
how Mary Lou moved and how (I think) she never knew.

A Lesson Learned from *Our Miss Brooks*

The second all-school play at West Linn High
Was taken from the screwball TV show
About a mouthy English teacher and the shy
Biology instructor who is slow
To pick up on the fact that she is all-
Consumed with making him her steady beau.
The girl who plays Miss Brooks is six feet tall,
The boy who plays Phil Boynton, six-foot-three.
(Boynton also coaches basketball.)
I have a minor role, which means I'm free
To lounge about and watch the others hone
Their skills. Then Mr. Liberty picks me
As Boynton's understudy. Seeds are sown
For utter chaos—and they bloom eight days
Before we open: Boynton's boy has flown!
I wonder, can an actor paraphrase
His lines? Ad lib when he forgets a word
Or two? Break into song? My cheeks ablaze,
I enter left—and sail on, undeterred,
Until Act Three, when I move in to kiss
Miss Brooks. Here's where it turns absurd.
In dress rehearsal, we skipped over this.
She's inches taller. I stand on my toes,
The only way to consummate our bliss.
The laughter's low at first, but then it grows.
Miss Brooks and I just stand there, eye to eye
And nose to nose, then lock lips like old pros.

Camp Hancock

Summer of 1951

The *Oregon Journal* item was so small
That only sharp-eyed readers would have seen
It nestled in among the ads—a call
For high school science students, boys between

Grades nine and twelve, to pitch in and create
A Central Oregon science camp designed
To give kids hands-on know-how in a slate
Of subjects. Leave it to my mom to find

The article and clip it out. She knew,
As did my dad, that I was born to dig
Up fossil dinosaurs. Out of the blue,
When I was five, I said when I was big

I would be famous for the fossil bones
I'd found. They even took me camping once
To John Day Fossil Beds State Park, known
For its mammal bones. I proved a dunce.

I had fun climbing up and down the green
And white formations of volcanic ash
That poured forth in the Early Oligocene,
But came up empty-handed, with heat rash.

The expedition's leader, Lon Hancock,
Considered Oregon's foremost fossil sleuth,
Was known worldwide for how he could unlock
Deep secrets underfoot. A rhino tooth

He found in the Clarno Nut Beds put to rest
The false belief drilled into expert heads:
No mammals in Oregon's Eocene. The best
Was yet to come—the Hancock Mammal Beds!

Fourteen of us signed on. The *Journal* sent
A photog out to shoot us, then we climbed
Aboard two Travelalls and off we went,
Adventure in our sails. We all were primed

And ready for whatever came our way.
When we arrived, sagebrush was what we found,
And juniper trees. We had a field day
Moving rocks and smoothing out the ground,

Erecting squad-size Army tents, setting
Up our cots inside, and stowing gear.
It wasn't all that hot, but we were sweating
Buckets. I was the first to volunteer

To make a run for water from a spring
Three miles away. A member of the staff
And I dipped scoops from deep inside the ring
Of algae, filling milk cans. He made me laugh,

The way he raved about the spotted bat.
He said we'd go at twilight to a cave
Where thousands thrived. We'd see their habitat
And learn about their ways. "And if you're brave

You'll hunker at the mouth as they pour out
In their nightly search for insects, a jet black
Cloud in motion, fluttering about—
And if you're lucky, hear their clickety-clack."

We strained the water through a muslin strip
And boiled it on the makeshift kitchen's chrome
And cast iron cook stove. When cool, I took a sip—
As sweet as water from our well at home.

Berrie Hancock, always with her hair
Up in a net and always apron-clad,
Kept staff and campers fed, with food to spare,
Three meals a day for twenty-four, and glad

We were—the food was great! When she and Lon
Came over on their fossil hunting jaunts,
She drove so he could keep a sharp eye on
Road cuts and talus slopes. Their needs and wants

Were few. Their lives revolved around the quest
For unknown knowledge of the distant past.
Our days were full. Lon put us to the test.
We sometimes fell behind, he walked so fast.

Rock hammers at the ready, we explored
Tuffaceous sandstone outcrops, pyroclastic
Flows, the works, and we were never bored.
My treasure from the nut beds was fantastic—

Agatized pecans, black walnuts, wood
With tunnels bored by teredo worms and filled
With calcite. I'd show Lon, and he'd say "Good,
Now what do you think it is?" and I'd be thrilled

When I got it right. One day he planted sticks
Of dynamite and blew a boulder from
The nut bed cliff, and rocks the size of bricks
Rained down. Though most showed nothing, there were some

With clustered nuts, undamaged by the fall.
My rucksack bulged as I dropped down the trail
To camp. I couldn't wait to spread my haul
Out—something we did daily, without fail.

Another time he blasted on a high
Formation close to camp where leaves were
Packed together tightly. My mind's eye
Envisioned fossils fit for a connoisseur.

I scrambled up and crept along a ledge
No wider than my hips—until I stepped
On something squishy. There, at the very edge,
Lay a four-foot western rattlesnake! I leapt

Straight back and landed on my feet. Good thing—
A talus slope peaked fifty feet below.
I hollered down for Nature Boy to bring
His hook and box. The snake was sluggish, so

The rest was easy. Driving home to Lake
Grove, Mom inquired, "What is that in the box?"
I said, "It's Russell, my pet rattlesnake."
She seemed calm, but I knew the look. "Rocks

And fossils, fine. But a rattlesnake?" My first
Act was to place the box in the living room
And block the doors. My next act was the worst
Blow to my pride: "Call Nature Boy, assume

He'll take the snake, and set a time, like soon."
So back to Portland. I was in free fall.
But Nature Boy maintained a snake commune
In his back yard. It turned out best for all.

Model Airplanes

I spent most rainy winter weekends locked
Away with tissue, balsa struts, and glue,
Constructing model airplanes. Peers were shocked
At how I slipped the grip of their purview,
Preferring to be cloistered with my vice,
A recluse with a safety razor blade
Perfecting craft and art. I once thought twice
Of my design, but then, decision made,
Instead of tethering their maiden flights,
A puppet master tugging at their strings,
I sent them soaring forth to see the sights,
To hug the wind and stretch their static wings.
The archaeologists who find my planes
Will ponder in their cups and scratch their brains.

The Wild Bunch

Away, away, from men and towns,
To the wild wood and the downs.
—Percy Bysshe Shelley

Like a literary Billy The Kid,
I packed Keats down the halls
of Lake Oswego High, sometimes
Shelley or a leather-bound Lord Byron,
sparking crackbrained mirth among
my jack-a-dandy peers, and sighs
from Bible types who nonetheless
shied from my beatitude.

Like a literary James Gang,
we strode slick green linoleum
between sheer hallway walls,
eyes glued to a far horizon
where deeds danced two-step
to a minuet, and arms crooked
lightly against a sudden draw
melted many a cast platitude.

Like a literary Wyatt Earp,
I silenced critics of my strange
behavior, quoting Keats, Shelley
or Lord Byron on the run, confounding
troglodytes with *St. Agnes' Eve*—
Ah, bitter chill it was! or, lightly,
On with the dance! let joy be unconfined!
as my reward for a little latitude.

Biting the Cigar

for Donald Spencer, playwright and director

Sir James M. Barrie let his hair way down when
he penned *Dear Brutus,* a takeoff on Shakespeare's
A Midsummer Night's Dream, set in Barrie's time.
I play Matey the Butler, properly stiff in the first
act, but looser than a gaggle of geese in the second.

We're guinea pigs in Mr. Spencer's thesis for his
Master of Arts in Theatre degree from Northwestern
University. The title translates roughly as *Methodology
in Transforming Minimally Gifted High School Players
into Fully Professional Thespians in One Trimester.*

Cast members must learn two distinct English accents—
a dozen actors learning half-a-dozen accents with no cross
pollination. We work in one pair for one accent, another
pair for another. Pairs segue into quartets. Dress rehearsal
is the first time we appear together. We don't disappoint.

We scratch our heads afterwards—wonder what it was
that left us so profoundly altered. Opening night jitters
vanish. The curtain rings down to thunderous applause.
Act One is a hit! I can hardly wait for Act Two, where
I woo Lady Caroline on a picnic blanket in the woods.

But I become a footnote in the thesis. I say, "Wait till
I light this cigar." She says, "Let me hold the darling
match." On cue I bite the tip off—way beyond what's
called for in the script. I spit and pick tobacco from my
lips as I sputter, "Tidy-looking Petitey Corona, this."

Mr. Spencer scribbles in his handy pad: *No detail too small to entrust to fate. Make Matey bite as many cigars as it takes until he gets it right.* At Saturday's matinee I pop the sucker off and sail it into the wings, the drama honorary, Masque and Dagger, my reward.

Immortal Prose

for Laurence Pratt, poet and mentor

In youth I viewed Elizabethan prose
As something of a Sisyphean task
That teachers of sadistic bent impose,
Their lust concealed behind a mummer's mask.
I feared complete antithesis of need
When Hamlet took possession of my sight,
For I expected heavy thought and deed
Devoid of phrases turned to my delight.
From that time on, my life's begun anew
With each successive reading of *Macbeth,*
Love's Labour's Lost, The Taming of the Shrew,
And, through my tears, the scene of Hamlet's death—
Immortal prose professors still require
In hopes of setting souls like mine afire.

My Heart Belongs to Only You

I was a Kenton fan from age ten on,
caught him every time he came to town,
bought all his albums, all his 45s,
knew all his sidemen by their instruments,
their names and faces, all his vocalists.

I was fifteen when I struck solid gold.
June Christy signed to do the Kenton tour.
I copped a ticket to a sold-out house—
The man ahead of me had turned his in!
Center section, sixth row, on the aisle.

I was first in line backstage, where Stan,
I fantasized, would knows me from his last
few gigs at Civic Auditorium.
I hugged the shadows as adoring fans
filed through. The first one in, the last to leave.

That's when the miracle occurred. A phone
rang in the wings, a stagehand picked it up.
Uh-huh. Okay. I'll let them know. G'bye.
Their flight was postponed due to heavy fog.
Instead of griping, they kicked back and jammed.

A tall stool beckoned me to center stage.
I was their audience—they played for me.
June Christy took my hands and moved in close.
Her bright eyes sparkled. I could feel her warmth.
My bones dissolved when she began to sing

My heart belongs to only you
I never loved as I love you
You've set a flame within me burning
A flame to stay within me yearning
It's just for you I want to live

I caught the early morning's last Blue Bus
before it cleared the Greyhound Station door
and rode alone in darkness through the fog.
    You are the song within my soul
    A melody that can't grow old

Sports

Basketball was not my strongest suit.
I liked the satin shorts and undershirt
But never learned to dribble worth a hoot.

Football made no sense to me. It hurt
To fling my body at a ten-ton truck
And wind up flattened, face-first in the dirt.

Baseball didn't bring me better luck.
For hours I'd stand around and scratch my crotch,
Then when a ball was popped my way, I'd duck.

Track and field held promise, but I'd botch
The simplest task. I couldn't meet demands
To beat the water boy. Still, I could watch,

And yell my head off. I could clap my hands
And stomp my feet. I found my forte—to root
Like crazy, raise the roof and rock the stands.

Courtney Newman's Five Olympic Golds

Camp Meriwether, Summer of 1952

T.J. was too spineless for his spit-
Polished colleague, who was military-
Minded as to discipline—so they split.

Old-Blood-and-Guts wore shorts and long socks, hairy
Knees exposed, forced rank and file to stand
Ramrod stiff. "Makes you men!" Contrary,

T.J. stood at ease despite demands
To tidy up his act. He walked. I jumped
Ship in his wake, to fill my sails, expand

Horizons. Before I knew it I was bumped
To Assistant Scoutmaster, Troop One-Twenty-Nine,
Chartered in Oswego. T.J. trumped

His Lake Grove rival, Mr. Rise-and-Shine.
Now he needed Scouts. My task, recruit
A bunch of twelve-year-olds, have parents sign

Permission slips, teach them how to salute.
I drafted Brother Cap, ranked Second Class,
Whose gift of gab made it a turkey shoot.

In no time he'd enrolled his friends en masse,
Dangling lures like "Two weeks away from your folks
At a camp on the Oregon Coast." Who could pass

That up? For the timid ones he had to coax,
He threw in "swimming, boating, running through breakers
On the golden sand below Cape Lookout," told jokes,

Cajoled the holdouts, turned them into takers.
Cap fashioned a woolly unit, packing the rolls
With a dozen fellow Lower Division Lakers.

Before we went to camp, they met some goals:
Made Tenderfoot as a group, stopped talking back,
Cracking wise, and peeing on campfire coals.

We covered needs beforehand, what to pack,
What not to pack, and how to pack it tight.
"You'll make do with the stuff in your haversack,"

I emphasized, recalling an oversight
My first time out: I forgot my underwear.
"Prepare for poison oak and bugs that bite."

We lucked out, snared the Viking campsite where
Old Blunderbuss himself played Cock of the Rock,
A stone's throw from the lake, beyond compare.

No sooner there than T.J. looked like chalk.
Beads of sweat popped from his brow. Eyes red,
Nose runny, he took to his cabin, said not to knock

Unless disaster struck. I tried to clear my head,
Sweep the cobwebs from my plastered vault.
My compass needle spun. I drowned in dread.

Not known for poise, I wasn't worth my salt.
Being suddenly thrust upstairs to leader
Was like a shift in the San Andreas fault.

I was a fifteen-year-old bottom feeder
In terms of what I knew. I could tell apart
A Sitka spruce and a Port Orford cedar,

Show some second graders how to start
A campfire without matches, but the gift
Of taming rowdy twelve-year-olds, an art

Mastered by few, escaped. My trial was swift.
"Fall in!" I shouted. Hubbub filled my ears.
"Fall out!" yelled Mole, to merriment. Adrift,

I faced a sea of fiendish grins. New fears
Clutched at my throat. The opening grew thinner
By the minute. Revved up, shifting gears,

I shouted, "Rot in hell! I'm going to dinner!"
And stomped off toward the mess hall half a mile
Away, bogged down by doubts. Was I the winner

Of our little squabble, or did Mole beguile
His mates with his rapier wit? *What if I fail?*
What if they starve to death? I swallowed a smile

When I glanced back, ten yards up the trail,
And spotted the Vienna Choir Boys
Padding after in bright dust draped like a veil,

Haloes glowing like neon Tinker Toys,
Single file through ferns and salal beneath
Red cedars in the setting sun. Some joys

Spring from anxieties—flip the wreath
Of gloom and find a shiny underside.
I dropped my shield, my spear, my sword and sheath,

My angst, and put some purpose in my stride.
They worked on merit badges. Days flew past.
We swam, had laughs around the campfire, tied

Knots till we were silly. The die was cast.
What happened next was a complete surprise.
I'd placed my tenderfooted charges last

In the Annual Meriwether Olympics, size
And inexperience and all, and they swept
Gold—the Meriwether Best Troop Prize.

"Butterfly?" I queried. Courtney leapt,
Flexing biceps, what little he owned of muscle
Making the high school state champ look inept,

Doing the breaststroke like a frog. His hustle
In the race across the lake, paddling hard right,
Entangled the other canoe-ers in a tussle.

Three more times he came in first, despite
The odds against winning when you've never done
The sport before, or professed even a slight

Interest. Arnold Southwell had his fun—
The smallest of us all zipped up and down
The greased pole in a flash. I fired a gun,

Something I hadn't wished to try, and found
The target's bull's-eye time and time again,
Though I didn't like the smell, or worse, the sound.

"Fall in!" I barked when T.J. left his den.
"Ten-*hut!*" Reviewing his recruits, he hit
The mark: "At ease. Congratulations, men."

The Still

Camp Hancock, Summer of 1952

Having time to kill before lights out,
We kick back on our cots and swap tall tales.
Tex, who speaks in low tones, talks about

His family's cattle ranch, how he stacks bales
Of hay six high on flatbed trucks, and rides
A horse to school most days. The kid who hails

From Canada, we call him Mouse, confides
He's scared to death of rattlesnakes. I scratch
My tale of Nature Boy's snake pit. Tex hides

A smile. Instead I tell about the batch
Of hooch I meant to make by soaking dried
Fruit with some yeast mixed in. The only catch

Was, when the mash began to fizz, I tried
To vent it with a rubber tube. Big flaw.
The tube got clogged. The cask blew up. I died

When I peeked inside the storage room and saw
Mom's canning jars, the ceiling and the floor,
The walls, all splattered with debris. "Hee-haw,"

Laughs Tex. "I never heard of that before!"
On the next day's run to Fossil for supplies,
We tag along. I hit the hardware store

For copper tubing. Tex and Mouse disguise
Their mission at the Safeway, where one shops
For a box of sugar while the other buys

A cake of yeast. My cashier knocks the props
From under me: "You plan to build a still?"
I cringe, and hope he doesn't call the cops.

Back at camp, we climb a nearby hill
And choose a spot that gets full sun all day.
We pick a bunch of juniper berries, fill

My metal war surplus canteen halfway,
Add water, sugar, yeast, give it a shake.
Tex coils the copper tube, and makes it stay

In the canteen's mouth with tape. A piece of cake.
The canteen cup will catch the alcohol,
Drip by drip. That night, we lie awake,

Brimming with success. "I had a ball!"
Mouse warbles. "Turn the volume down," I hush.
"That was a bit of all right," Tex says, his drawl

Drawn out. Next morning, after chow, we rush
Back up the hill to where the canteen sits.
No action yet. We circle it with brush

To cut the copper's glitter. Tex admits
The obvious: "These things take time." We wait.
Days pass. When we're about to call it quits,

The drops start dripping at a rapid rate.
We grin, agree to sneak off when the coast
Is clear that evening, set to celebrate.

The cup's half full. "I'd like to make a toast,"
Says Tex. "Let's hear it for the Musketeers!"
Mouse takes a sip, looks like he's seen a ghost,

Flutters off down the hill and disappears
Over a crest. In a heartbeat, we hear cries
And laughter from the trail below. "Cheers,"

Says Tex. He slurps a nip. I recognize
The voices—female campers. Taking turns,
We pass the cup, and soon, tears fill my eyes,

My legs go wobbly, and my stomach churns.
"I'm through," I say. "The rest is yours, my friend."
Tex stretches out. "I will admit it burns

My lips and throat, but I won't try to pretend—
This here's the best moonshine, without a doubt,
I ever tasted. Good to the bitter end."

Eocene Bonanza

Clarno Nut Beds, Camp Hancock, Summer of 1952

Three days, from dawn to sundown, Jack and I
Hammer chisels in the thin black seam
That runs around the boulder, shoulder high.
Sweat stings our eyes, our muscles ache. My dream
Is treasure, his is knowledge, though the role
Of disentombing life wrapped up in rock
For fifty million years defines a goal
We share—the truth and beauty we'll unlock.
Third night, by lantern light, we press ahead.
The seam pops open with a crackling sound.
We pound some wooden wedges in, to spread
The blocks and get a look at what we've found.
The fossil nuts that glitter in the gloom
Rival the golden horde of King Tut's tomb.

*for Jack Wolfe, who won a Merit Scholarship for
an essay based on his Camp Hancock experience,
graduated* summa cum laude *from Harvard, and,
having switched his major from nuclear physics,
went on to become a distinguished paleobotanist*

Six:

Battle of the Strippers

Battle of the Strippers

Portland Mayor Dorothy McCullough Lee, known as
"No Sin Lee" for the way she chop-chopped Chinese
gambling dens, rode into office in 1948 on a pledge
to sanitize the vice-ridden city. Brothels, strip joints,
bars and clubs fell before her juggernaut. Four years
later, Mayor Fred Peterson strode in and everything
returned to normal, with not one, but two burlesque
theaters opening downtown, the Star at NW 3rd and
Burnside, and the Capitol at SW 4th and Morrison.

Don spread the red-hot news all over school:
The shows that afternoon would be obscene!
Candy Renee and Tempest Storm would duel

To see who reigned as Portland's burlesque queen.
The last false claims to modesty would drop.
He'd heard details of Candy's new routine

Where suddenly a tasseled pastie pops,
The curtain closes with a rush, the comic zooms
Onstage all flummoxed while the plainclothes cops

Scowl and scratch their noggins. Business booms!
Don swore he heard the story word for word
While lounging backstage by the dressing rooms.

Knowing Don, that didn't seem absurd.
He always seemed to have the inside scoop.
As on our past excursions, he chauffeured,

Six guys crammed inside his two-door coupe.
We headed off at noon. To pass time while
We waited, Don dragged Broadway, did the loop.

Soon I sat front row on the center aisle
So close I saw the pores on the comic's nose
As he cracked wise, his nicotine-stained smile.

I was amazed to see that all the rows,
Main floor and balcony, were filled with boys
Of high school age and men in dapper clothes.

Those whose sex lives hinged on flicks and toys
Were there, as well as titans and tycoons.
You couldn't talk for all the background noise.

Candy Renee pranced out with a bunch of balloons
And a hat pin, *Pop-pop-pop*. Her pasties clung
To her nipples, hanging there like crescent moons.

All eyes were frozen open. Springs were sprung.
She had us worked to a froth. The climax came—
A pastie dropped. The gauntlet had been flung!

The Star went crazy. Candy's crafty game
Raised hoots and hollers, whistles, claps and cheers.
In a flash the curtain closed. The comic's lame

Routine had to do with buffalos and steers
But no one heard the punch line. Out the door
And up the street we charged as one, our fears—

That someone else would get in line before
Us, or we wouldn't get in at all—in vain.
I wound up front row, center aisle, main floor.

When Tempest Storm sashayed onstage my brain
Shot ripples down my spine and tipped my chair
As if I had been hit by a speeding train.

Her eyes were clear and bright, and oh, her hair—
A flaming torch from tiers of overhead lights
With gels—her skin both luminous and fair—

And oh, her breasts—devoured in tiny bites
By hordes of adoring fans. Her forty-four
Double-Ds uncupped—twin swans whose flights

Of fancy soared. Not mimicry of whore
As Mayor "No Sin Lee" and ilk were taught—
Their training aimed at thou-shalt-not-adore-

The-human-body-viewed-as-finely-wrought—
But classic practice of an ancient art.
Her bosom mesmerized, her movements caught

Me in their ebbs and flows and broke apart
Like waves on a tropical shore, the water warm,
The air perfumed, humidity off the chart.

Both pasties flew—two points for Tempest Storm!—
But not before she'd twirled her tassels first
This way, then that, as if it were the norm

For breasts to be rotated, then reversed,
Then swung in orbits with opposing arcs.
I read that all her moves were unrehearsed,

She let her body sway until the sparks
Began to fly, then reeled the suckers in.
The tunas swooned, the dolphins flipped, the sharks

Went on a feeding frenzy. Through the din
That rose as pasties fell, I heard the screech
Of whistles. House lights flared—a loony bin

Was tame compared! We heard a speech
By Portland's top cop, Diamond Jim Purcell
Himself, bullhorn in hand, about this breach

Of decency we all had witnessed: "Hell
Is a preferable place to be!" Of course, he hung
Out at the Star, where Candy rang his bell,

So he would know. I wisely held my tongue.
Don told his crew to stick like glue, he'd lead
Us out. We slithered like a snake among

The patrons waiting, willing to concede
Defeat. Beneath the stage, behind the pit,
Don swung a small door wide. He guaranteed

Our safety through the passageway. "Don't split,
Stay cool, pay no attention to the rats."
Ten minutes later there appeared a slit

Of light. We stumbled on a clutch of cats
In an alley lined with smelly garbage cans—
Much better that a bunch of dicks with gats

And night sticks loading people into vans.
Don dubbed Tempest Storm a double wow,
A doll. Already he was making plans.

He went on about her knockers, how
He'd like to be a flea in her brassiere,
How he'd seen smaller udders on a cow.

The whole drive home I listened to him steer
The banter back to boobs. His terms for breast—
Bazooka, hooter, bumper, jug—made clear

That he was prematurely weaned, confessed
That he was starved for motherly love, in fact
Was what a Freudian would call obsessed.

While Don played joker, I rehearsed my act.
Once home, I had to face the music, trust
My parents wouldn't press me till I cracked.

They didn't know I skipped! I was nonplussed.
Instead of tethered to a ducking stool
I spent the night immersed in Tempest's bust.

Dances with Trigonometry

for Roy Hadley, math teacher extraordinaire

I struggled through two years of math before
It struck me that my teachers lacked pizzazz—
But then I stepped through Mr. Hadley's door
And trigonometry went razzmatazz,
The opposite of deadly dull. I soared!
He taught as if math were a love affair,
And mesmerized me with his boundless store
Of energy, his eagerness to share
The joys of graphs, identities, and more.
He bounced when he chalked figures on the board,
His eyes ablaze. He never met a chord
Or sphere he wouldn't unlock and explore.
I never dreamed that math could rank up there
With poetry and theater and jazz.

Summer of 1953

Got paid out on Monday
Ain't a dog soldier no more
They gimmee all this money
So much my pockets are sore
No more can I refuse
Re-enlistment Blues

The big movie that summer, *From Here to Eternity*, gave Jack Cedergreen and me hours of entertainment on the L.L. Rogers Ranch near Adams. We murdered *Re-enlistment Blues* before breakfast and after supper.

In between, we pitched cut pea vines into viners, stacked boxes of peas for the cannery trucks, and kept an eye out for Burly Balls, the foreman, who sat on nearby rises, shifting the focus on his binoculars and swigging Scotch, twenty-four hours a day, seven days a week, to keep him going.

Burly Balls played football at Oregon with Dad. Had he known Jack and I were aspiring writers in search of characters, plots, scenes, he never would have hired us.

What seemed at first like sport soon turned to drudgery. Rise before dawn. Dress in clothes you took to bed with you to avoid the shock of frozen shirts, pants and socks.

Breakfast soon after, stainless steel platters stacked with bacon, fried eggs, every cut of steak, rib, sirloin, tenderloin, from steers slaughtered twice a week. Climb aboard a man-jack truck for a bone-chilling half-hour ride to the day's field.

Twelve long, hot hours later, drag back with dirt-clogged nostrils, fireweed rash etched at wrists and neck, and wrinkled feet from the ground pea vine juice that seeped into waterproof boots. Wait in line at the shower shack. Eat. Shoot the breeze. Hit the sack.

Thursdays were liver and onion days—not uncommon for rabid fans to suffer fork wounds in the mad scramble.

We pitched with Mickey, the only other high school kid on the ranch. We talked about the straw bosses, pea-dinks, bulldozer operators, the schoolteacher who drove the lunch wagon, the three Indian girls who drove the Model A dump trucks that dropped pea vines before the ancient viners.

We spoke in general terms about the girls, how much fun it was to flirt with them across the truck runway or when luck-of-the-draw put them in front of our viner, how great it would be if we could connect.

After it rained we took advantage of the one-day break and walked into Adams. All there was to the town was a skinny two-story brick general store, a scattering of small houses, some unoccupied, and an old four-room schoolhouse with a wrought iron swing set and teeter-totters out front.

We lounged in the swings, discussing the girls, when all of a sudden, like a scene from some movie, there they were, walking toward us up the dusty street, the afternoon light shimmering behind them. The pairing was preordained. Walking them back down the street, we held hands, Ruth and I, Jack and Josephine, Mickey and Juanita.

We made plans to meet next evening at a spot on Wildhorse Creek where the bank was flat and grassy. I was in charge—I knew how to build a campfire and had fake I.D., the result of Dad's old Remington having the same typeface and size used on Oregon driver's licenses. I pasted a 2 over the 7 in 1937, increasing my age to 21, then slipped the license into a plastic sleeve. Voila!

Campfire built, case of Oly hidden in a thicket, blankets spread in scattered locations, we waited. They lived along Wildhorse Creek in a tent camp with their grandmother and assorted aunts, uncles and cousins, all of whom worked for the L.L. Rogers spread during summer harvests.

Again they materialized out of nowhere. Ruth and I sat on a blanket near the blazing fire, exchanging smiles. Her eyes were deep and tinged with mystery. Touching her hand sent tingles down my spine.

We shared a beer, then kissed. I wrapped my jacket around her shoulders as the air took on a chill, the fire burned low. We talked, stopping whenever whoops and laughter burst from the flickering shadows. Kissing was a sometimes thing charged with electricity.

A week later, another downpour, another free day. The girls borrowed Grandmother's four-door sedan. We all chipped in, bought a case of Oly, and spent the afternoon swimming in the Umatilla River, sunning on the sand.

Grandmother, wise to the beer, phoned the sheriff. Ruth had told an aunt and uncle where we'd be. They came out to warn us, told us to meet them later at a crossroads if we needed help.

I was behind the wheel when red lights flashed in the rearview mirror. We swung into a sharp curve with no shoulders. I spotted a wide-open barbed-wire gate and pushed the gas pedal to the floor.

We shot up twin tracks—no braking or the ponderous car would settle to its underpinnings in the thick dust—until we reached a crest. Below us stretched opposing rows of viners operating under floodlights.

The county cops stayed tight on my tail right to the point where I committed to splitting the rows, to shooting through, hoping pea-dinks would muster enough strength to leap out of the way. The cops peeled off.

A half-mile later, the clutch froze, jammed with dust. We abandoned the car, headed for the crossroads where the aunt and uncle said they'd meet us, and cringed in a roadside ditch while a trucker checked his load, so close we could see up his pant legs.

The aunt and uncle showed up. We crammed into their back seat and hid under blankets until we reached Adams. The girls went back to camp, we high-tailed it for the ranch.

Early next morning, Ike, a straw boss, warned us the FBI was on our case. Furnishing alcohol to Indians was a federal offense. We drew our pay, grabbed our backpacks, and ran across a fallow field, keeping the barn between us and the two black sedans rumbling down the mile-long driveway, roiling plumes of dust.

The rancher who picked us up kept his mouth shut through state and county roadblocks, and dropped us in Athena, where we hid in the city park. Late that afternoon, Jack and Mickey took off to scope out the Greyhound depot and buy some food. We hadn't eaten since the day before.

I stashed our gear in the bushes and climbed a tree. After dark, county cops cruised through three times. Spotlights skimmed my boot soles.

Jack and Mickey finally showed up. They told me they had avoided two tough-looking city cops at the bus depot. The stuff they bought was pure carbohydrate, except for the deep-fried pork rinds. Their drink of choice: Orange Crush.

We snuck out of town early the next morning, hitched a ride north to College Place, Washington, where Mickey's mom and stepdad lived in Hell's Half-Acre, in a basement with the first floor as a roof. The stepdad played banjo with a cigarette stuck to his lower lip.

Jack and I plotted our next move: We would head south, make our way to Jamaica, work on fishing boats, and write.

Passing through Athena, we spotted Grandmother's sedan on a service station rack and paid for towing and a new clutch, leaving us with less than a hundred bucks apiece for all that back-breaking, mind-numbing labor.

We caught a ride to The Dalles and stared long and hard at the US 97 south-to-California sign. And what then? Jack opted for a straight shot home. I set my sights on Adams, and Ruth.

Grandmother had called off the cops. Burly Balls hired me back, though I couldn't live at the ranch. I took a cot in a tent at the Indian camp, now split between young and old, thanks to us. Ruth and I spent blissful off-hours together.

After the peas played out, I stayed on and drove a double electric axle dump truck in the wheat harvest, learned fast how to dance with undulating combines over shifting landscapes, the mating of two huge machines. The slightest slip-up would shower my windshield with grain and escalate the header-puncher's cussing skills. I closed out the season at the grain elevator in Adams, boarding up and filling boxcars in heat that raised blisters on my back.

Ruth and I made our goodbyes in a stubble field a short hop from camp, under a wide sky thick with stars, wandering hand in hand, searching for words. The world looked different. My life was changed. I loved with a tentative sense of what love was, loved someone I might never see again. But I loved.

*
**

Epilogue

Ike got weekends off, spent Friday nights getting ready, stepped from the shower looking like a boiled lobster, took an hour in front of the mirror slicking back hair on both sides of the naked noggin he buffed with a shoeshine rag, clipping his nose hairs, tweezing between his eyebrows.

Dressed in checkered cowboy shirt with pearl snaps, freshly pressed Wranglers turned up ten inches at the cuff, wide leather belt, fancy silver buckle buffed to a fare-thee-well, he'd rise to his full height, five-foot-four in his spit-polished cowboy boots, and declare himself "hot to trot."

Off he'd drive in his custom baby-blue Ford pickup, off to The Waldorf, one of several upstairs whorehouses along Walla Walla's main drag, for a date with a woman he'd been seeing for fifteen years.

He delivered his favorite saying, "That's a good deal, that ain't bad," like Pa Kettle with a dash of W.C. Fields thrown in. His theme song was *Bummin' Around.*

I got an old slouch hat
Got my roll on my shoulder
I'm as free as a breeze
An' I'll do as I please
Just a bummin' around

Playing Hardball with the Broadway Boys

I don't remember what my brother Cap
Said to get the goat of the Broadway Boys.
I only know that like a sudden clap

Of thunder, all about me there was noise,
Loud shouts, those things that middle fingers say.
While Cap and friends, the Seven Little Foys

I'd ferried to the Great White Way to play,
Pretended they had never seen my mug,
I warbled, "We'll be on our merry way,"

And piled the blighters in the back seat, snug
As bugs. I peeled rubber down the block,
And squealed a corner on two wheels. The thugs

Hugged bumpers with me while my cackling flock
Of morons made weird faces and guffawed.
Macadam Avenue. I heard a knock.

A car guy said "Sounds like a piston rod."
A service station loomed. No soul in sight.
Better we should face a firing squad

Than let a pack of jackals take delight
Tap-dancing on our foreheads. We were caught
Between a hard place and a rock. To fight

Or not to fight was moot. I'd never fought
For real before. The Broadway Boys piled out
And circled like a school of sharks, red-hot

And ready, switch-blade knives for teeth, no doubt
A preview of our fast-approaching fate.
I had a thought. Their honcho was about

To smash my window. With my chin as bait,
I rolled the window down. He swung his fist.
I ducked and rolled the window up. Checkmate.

He tried to wriggle out—man, he was pissed!
I shifted, popped the clutch, gave it the gas.
His hand wrenched free. His watch flew from his wrist

And landed in the back seat, where Cap's class-
Mates laughed their fool heads off. The booby trap
They sprung on me was just a lark—my ass.

The Unflappable Mademoiselle Proulx

I laugh to think of Eva Proulx
Who kept her classroom windows closed
For fear she would contract the flu.

The thought that she might be exposed
To viruses and other stuff
Gave her the chills. I was opposed

To stale air, so I called her bluff
One hot spring day—strolled in before
Class, raised a window. Sure enough,

The minute she walked through the door,
She slammed the window shut. The room
Grew warmer. What I had in store

For her—skunk cabbage in full bloom
Between her cushion and her chair—
Soon filled her space with rank perfume.

Surely she would seek fresh air,
I thought, and throw the windows wide—
But no, she stoically sat there

And took the pungent scent in stride!
My classmates chuckled and guffawed
Behind their books, as mystified

As I was at her stone façade.
I felt I'd met my Waterloo,
The victim of an act of God.

Bronze Bosom above Teak and Mahogany Inboard Runabout

Colleen's good fortune was her family's wealth,
Enabler of her vintage runabout,
Her cocoa-butter tan, her teeth, her health,
The extra pounds she packed from dining out—
No criticism of the extra pounds
That gravitated to her splendid chest
And made her bosom spill its bounds,
An invitation to imagine her undressed.
I was the startled one when she swapped ends
And throttled down, making her runabout bob,
Her heavenly bosom bathed—the thought transcends—
In shimmering light. "New nose?" I said. "Nice job."
I don't aspire to dabble in her league.
My light is beeswax candle, hers is klieg.

Born to Be Bearded

The whole affair began with a dare
To see who could grow the best beard.
Steeple bells pealed, the rally squad squealed
And Principal Belknap sneered.

The bells may be hyperbole,
But the rest of the tale rings true.
What we had done was make a run
At a sacrosanct taboo.

"Hirsute's a look in a history book—
Lincoln, Whitman, Thoreau.
No high school student who's halfway prudent
Allows facial hair to grow."

I heard the peals as well as the squeals
And watched as the principal leered.
Nothing at all had held me in thrall
Like the prospect of growing a beard.

We stood forty strong at the starting gong,
All aiming to finish first.
Within a few days we had entered the phase
Where bubbles begin to burst.

Some dropped because they discovered fuzz
Was all their chins could muster.
Others cracked after thoroughly whacked
By girlfriend, parents, pastor.

The urge to scratch their prickly thatch
Drove many to scrape their faces.
Others fell victim to edict and dictum
And suffered untold disgraces.

I boasted a growth that was lauded both
For fullness and for effect.
I was the loner who flipped a boner—
What the principal dubbed *Disrespect*.

I loved to strut the halls and jut
My jaw at all who gaped.
Miss Barbey was a prize because
One glance and she felt undraped.

I was the fool who mocked her rule
Over the senior class—
As if *Advisor* made her the wiser
And less of a horse's ass.

She, to be fair, though I didn't share
Her spit-polished-boot way of thinking,
Ran a taut ship where fear of a slip
Kept many a soul from sinking.

At first I wondered if I had blundered
Somehow in her drill-sergeant eyes.
Then it dawned on me—I was born to be free,
A type she was born to despise.

On a Friday night, by the full moon's light,
While my date and I were drowned
In suds in the back of my rattletrap,
The contest winner was crowned.

I spent the weekend up the creek
Nursing my downsized ego.
I'd blown my chance to sing and dance
As the hero of Lake Oswego.

All was not lost. I weighed the cost
Of tossing my razor for keeps.
What could they do?—other than skew
My odds in the scholarship sweeps.

Thin-veiled threats from teachers' pets
Failed to pop my balloon.
I chose to wait and trust to fate.
The showdown came Friday, high noon.

Principal Belknap, mad as hell,
Made it abundantly clear:
"Come Monday morn, if your beard isn't shorn,
You're out on your ear, you hear?"

Belknap was tough. He'd called my bluff.
What could I do but crumble?
Without a prod I gave him a nod
And a barely audible mumble.

I spent the weekend cheek to cheek
With Merry and sister Mirth,
Whose lively chatter settled the matter.
Concede? No way on Earth!

Come Monday morn, the clarion horn
Sounded a softer tone.
Living to fight for what was right,
I tossed Belknap his bone.

A Narrow Escape

With graduation just around the bend, Jack Cedergreen and I agree we have some heavy reminiscing to do. Our pea harvest adventures. Our immersion in rhythm and blues when everyone else was content to hum along with Doris Day and Perry Como. Our famous *You Can't Take It with You* cast party.

With four quarts of Miller High Life in hand, we hop in my '38 Ford on a cloudless Saturday night and head for Skylands, where I beat the West Linn High chug-a-lug champ. I tell Jack the story as we snake up the gravel road to the top.

We stop at a spot with a sweeping view of Portland lights to the north. The party springs to the fore. I played Tony Kirby, the romantic lead, but Jack had the livelier role—Mr. De Pinna, the iceman who showed up at the Sycamore house nine years before and stayed to help make fireworks in the basement.

As usual, the party was held at the home of a cast member whose parents were out of town. Everyone was schnockered by the time some kid burst in and shouted, "The cops are on their way!" Needless to say, pandemonium reigned.

The house was perched on a steep slope a couple of hundred feet above Oswego Lake. A cast member climbed over the deck railing before Jack and another guy pulled him to safety. I tried stuffing myself into a roll of linoleum in the garage.

Turned out it was a false alarm, and we returned to partying. My last act was to wheel the props manager to his front door in a Safeway shopping cart, ring the doorbell, and run like hell.

Our laughter is shattered by headlights blazing through the rear window. I start the engine and keep my hand on the stick shift nob. But the car backs up, turns around, and drives off.

We turn our attention to the pea harvest, the high times we had, our rendezvous along Wildhorse Creek, our romances with Ruth and Josephine, the wild cross-country car chase.

Again our laughter is broken by a pair of headlights. This time I start the car, pop the clutch and peel out, spraying gravel. In a flash, the headlights are joined by a revolving red light.

In my rear-view mirror, I recognize the brand new Dodge Red Ram V-8 Hemi that Clackamas County Sheriff's Deputy Fred Abel showed off to admiring eyes at Lake Oswego High.

My '38 Ford is no match for a Red Ram V-8, but all I can think about is not getting caught with beer. Away we go, down the narrow, winding gravel road, headlights off, staying in third gear as a substitute for braking.

"Toss the beer!" I yell. Jack rolls down his window, pitches the four bottles, two full and two half-empty, out onto the road. We start to fishtail. I tap the brakes.

I recognize the utter absurdity of our situation. Turning on the lights, I shift into low, brake to a stop, and roll down my window. "As you know," Deputy Abel says calmly, "the legal age to drink in Oregon is twenty-one. Are you twenty-one?"

"Give or take a few years," I quip.

"You boys are in a peck of trouble," he says, ignoring my smartass remark. "Minor in possession, reckless driving, and five or six lesser offenses."

"Don't you want to see my driver's license?"

"I know who you are." He scribbles on a pad, tears off a sheet, and hands it to me. "You and Jack will appear before a juvenile court judge at the appointed hour, accompanied by your parents." With that he climbs in his car and takes off.

"That's all?" I say, relieved.

"That's enough," says Jack. "My parents won't like this."

The judge is a very nice woman who speaks in a stern but pleasant voice, explaining the serious nature of what we did.

Jack and I nod every few seconds. When it comes our turn to speak, we promise to never again do anything so stupid.

"I trust this won't affect my shot at a Navy scholarship," I add, hoping to emerge with a clean record.

Five classmates have signed up for the four-hour scholarship exam. First thing Monday, I add my name to the list.

Miss Barbey

Miss Barbey stares at me in disbelief,
Re-reads the letter, double-checks my name.
Her battleship lays battered on a reef.

"You? A Navy scholarship? Good grief!"
My lot would blot her admiral brother's fame.
Miss Barbey stares at me in disbelief,

Picks up the phone receiver, dials the Chief
Of Naval Operations. Wracked with shame,
She, like her ship, lays shattered on the reef.

"Arleigh? Frances here. I have a beef!"
Her wrinkles bulldog deep, her cheeks aflame,
Miss Barbey glares at me in disbelief.

"The matter's cast in brass? In bold relief?
The Navy doesn't play a guessing game?"
Her looking glass lays scattered on the reef.

I jam her radar with my stealth. A thief,
I steal her compass, compromise her aim.
Miss Barbey stares at me in disbelief.
Her battle flag lays tattered on the reef.

A Day in the Life of a Pea-Dink: July 19, 1954

Prologue

I caught a quick glimpse of Ruth when I stopped by the camp on Wildhorse Creek, but three unsmiling young men let me know I wasn't welcome.

The harvest was late. The peas were slow to ripen, and ranchers weren't hiring, though they did set up a soup kitchen in Athena to keep workers around. Served the thinnest bean soup I ever tasted, lucky if I found a whole bean in a bowl.

The Presbyterian Church in Milton-Freewater laid out an array of game animals confiscated from poachers. Once a day I thumbed the twelve miles. Elk and venison mostly, but bear and bison cropped up. Locals donated fruit and vegetables.

Athena's three-man police force was stretched as thin as its bean soup. Fights broke out. There was a nasty brawl at Pike's Café. I watched two cops lounge across the street, leaning on their pickup, slapping their palms with foot-long leather saps filled with lead slugs, until a man staggered through the doors holding his guts in his hands, and they waded in.

I spent half an hour in the tiny stone jailhouse, a throwback to the nineteenth century, for stopping to look in the Rexall Drug Store window, a violation of the city's hastily drawn loitering ordinance. I was pushed out and halfway down the block to make room for six undocumented Mexicans.

The peas finally ripened. I joined pea-dinks gathered at the Associated station at 5:30 every morning, waiting to be waved aboard a man-jack truck.

*
* *

Dust drops like quicksilver from the wheels of the Model A trucks rolling in to dump loads of cut pea vines before rows of grinding viners on the plain outside Athena.

It is dawn. Nightshift workers take long-handled pitchforks

to the tangled vines as man-jack trucks, beds packed with dark forms huddled against the chill, lumber up and stop.

Day workers hop down to the truck runway, to the ground vines spread to minimize dust during the heat of the day.

Motors slow to a low growl as mechanics throw gear levers to idle the viners, and proceed to grease moving parts, unjam chain hoists, fill gas tanks, and repair broken belts.

Night workers shuffle to the foreman's truck to receive their checks for ninety-four cents an hour for twelve hours of pitching, minus fifty cents for lunch, and forty-seven cents for the half hour allowed for eating the two thin sandwiches and government surplus apple.

Day workers choose pitching partners with a glance and a nod, stamp feet against the cold, bend gloves around fork handles to work out the stiffness of dried pea vine juice and ground-in dirt. A few glance at the distant Blue Mountains, drawn like a saw blade across the dawn sky, but turn back from the new day's promise of clogged nostrils, cracked lips, and black spittle.

Engines roar, chipped gears whir, chain hoists clank, sounds that will tear at the minds of workers till they give themselves over, body and soul, to their machines.

Winos, bums, bindlestiffs, skid road down-and-outers, Okies, Mexican Nationals, Indians, the urban unemployed, all bring their tattered dreams to the fields and leave with the juice of crushed pea vines running in their veins.

Doc Ayres, chiropractor from Stillwater, Oklahoma who lived by his smarts for thirty-five years, turning a third-grade education into a successful medical practice. Caught, spent five years in the state pen. Survives as an elevator operator during lean times on the harvest circuit. Believes he can perform the work of three men half his age.

Wilbur Oka, Blackfoot from Alberta, old at twenty from having killed a man at seventeen in Korea. Hobbled from having both legs broken by a Cheyenne, Wyoming mob after capturing Best Bronc Rider at Frontier Days.

Luke Foss, "po' white" living in the Dust Bowl days of the Great Depression. Gripes about the "gummint," of which he is ignorant, and harvest work, which is all he knows, and which always pays better wages up the line. "Hear they's makin' 'leven dollar a day outen Walla Walla a piece."

Joselito Gonzales, Mexican from Waco, Texas, his home for five years since crossing the border. Works hard to finance bouts in the second-floor whorehouses along Walla Walla's main drag. Brings the latest whorehouse jokes to the fields.

Bo Charlie, toothless, hollow-eyed hobo who slips into the crowd milling about the Associated station parking lot. Takes pains to tell anyone who will listen the difference between hobos like himself and worthless, no-good bums and tramps.

Jamey Burke, All-American football player who carries his yellowed scraps of glory in the pocket of his faded denim shirt, behind a Bull Durham pouch. Garners the attention of winos with dago red before his tale ends in puke and tears.

Professor, who earned advanced degrees in three fields but couldn't hold onto a job. Poet-philosopher who one day found himself out West, following harvests, reading Shakespeare and Whitman, Plato and Homer in the original. Fancies himself the last true classical scholar, choosing the breadth of America as the sounding board for his postulations and pentameters.

Willy Democrat Jones, son of a "New O-leens niggah an' a bayou peddlah-man," who dances nightly at the truck barn for the colored drivers who haul boxes of shelled peas from viner to cannery, collecting enough pennies to buy a bowl of chili at Pike's Café after wiring his pay to his mother, who is unable to work "wid 'er stiff jernts an' swolled-up ligs."

These are a few of the men motioned onto a man-jack truck this July morning to pitch for the Preacher, a man of God who works peas six days of every harvest week, and tends his flock of saints on the seventh, letting a straw boss handle the Sunday hiring of sinners.

These are a few of the men who will sweat, burn, and die small deaths for the sin of having waked to live and work another day; who bend low, hands tucked in armpits, facing bone-biting wind on open benches during the long ride to the Preacher's field, but who soon forget cold even exists; who pray for a breeze to cool their backs, but tear at their shirts when a breeze comes with its fireweed needles.

I am here, fresh out of high school, a seasoned pea-dink in my second summer. Doc and Luke call me "Kid," assume I'm a greenhorn in need all the good advice they can give.

There is no whistle to signal the start of work, but the men know their efforts will ease as stiffness leaves their muscles and motions become automatic, and so each man begins in time with the man at the next viner on down the line, digging-lifting-swinging, pausing to make sure the chain hoist teeth grab the vines, swinging a second load before the first whips, thrashing, into the mouth of the spinning cylinder and down inside, where peas spill, and pods, vines and fireweed grind to a pulp ejected on an elevated belt at the back.

Four men work each pair of viners; two pitch two loads of vines between them, two box shelled peas and stack full boxes beside the viners; then they trade jobs, back and forth.

Cannery drivers park nearby and rest in the shade of their flatbed trucks, playing cards and singing and telling jokes while they wait for their first loads of boxes. When they back their rigs in, they make sure pea-dinks know just how little they work for their fourteen dollars a day.

"Sho' glad it you down in de pea soup, boy. You niggahs ought t' git a white man's job, like me."

As debris piles up behind the viners, bulldozers rumble into action, belching blue smoke as thick-necked operators pump throttles, jerk levers, scatter stacks of ground pea vines, and level the long mound. Spreader trucks slosh through the green sludge pooled between mound and viners, gathering debris to spit out over the ocean of dust plowed by waves of trucks bringing pea vines in from nearby fields.

The noise forces us to speak up when we have something to say, but we have little to say as a rule.

I work with Wilber, Doc and Joselito on a pair of viners. Doc is teamed with Wilber, and I'm teamed with Joselito. Doc and I pitch, Wilber and Joselito fill and stack boxes.

"Viners 're jest like wimmin," Doc grumbles over the din. "Pick one an' y' spend ever' wakin' hour wonderin' ef th' one on down th' line don't work a mite better."

At first he pitches two forks for every one of mine. But the stark contrast between my lean body and his slumped form, my seventeen years against his sixty-seven, causes him to first lighten his fork loads, then settle on one-for-one, and finally fake even that between frequent trips to the water barrel.

We finish a load with no loads waiting. Joselito uses the break to pile ground pea vines on the water barrel and sprinkle cups of water on top. Wilber uses the break to remove a field boot, shake out the dust, and cover a hole in the sole with the folded jacket of a pulp fiction. Doc uses the break to hit the outhouse. I use the break to stretch out in the sliver of shade beside the stacked boxes, pick caked dust from my nostrils, and stare at the pale blue sky.

The load arrives. Wilber and Joselito take to their forks, digging-lifting-swinging, forgetting the break had happened.

The sun rises higher as each load of vines disappears and another takes it place. Dust rises despite ground vines spread on the runway. Fireweed etches red rings at collars and cuffs, sticks to backs, burns from the friction of sweat-soaked shirts.

A dust devil dances along the runway. I grit my teeth, and hold my soiled bandana close over my mouth and nose until my breath softens it and it clings. Load replaces load, and stacks of empty boxes replace full ones on their way to the canneries at Pendleton, Athena, and Milton-Freewater.

A viner down the line idles, stops. The grinding and clanking cease as the other viners follow suit, leaving a loose silence awash with distant voices, a cough, water dripping into a tin cup under a tap, the sporadic buzzing of a fly dying at my feet, making angels in the dust.

Some men drop their forks, others lean on theirs, as the water Jeep bumps from viner to viner and the driver drops brown paper sacks as a guarantee that we last out the day.

It is noon. We have worked six hours, have six to look forward to, with thirty minutes for wolfing lunch and lying in a spot of shade if we can find one, and five and a half hours for breathing dust, drinking stale water, and spitting mud.

Luke joins Doc at the water barrel. They eat in silence while viner mechanics climb over the machines with outsized monkey wrenches, grease guns, gas cans, and oily rags, checking chain links, freshening lubrication points, kicking bent chain guards, pulling at vines snarled around gear arms.

Doc fills the water cup, and after drinking, drops in his dentures, rubbing them to remove dirt and bits of sandwich from between the teeth. He and Luke talk about the old days and the present day, harvest news from up in Walla Walla and over at Pocatello and Lewiston, and wages for picking apples at Hood River against what Yakima might pay.

Engines rev, gears mesh, the chair hoists clank to life, the huge cylinders spin. Doc and I pick at the tangled vines before tearing into them with a vengeance, as if the load before us is the last we'll pitch on this or any other day.

The pace slackens. We settle into a groove no different from the one that moved morning into afternoon, except we grew a day older at noon, and we will age another day before settling on our full bellies, our empty bottles, our dreams.

Doc complains of a bad heart he picked up in prison, of sons who "rightly shoulda made plans fer th' ol' man in 'is few remainin' years" and of daughters who deserted him.

"What's a man go 'n build up a fam'ly fer ef they packs up 'n leaves jest when he starts t' need 'em?" Daughters and sons who, he makes plain enough, received little comfort from him during the years when they had no one else to turn to.

Wilber talks about how it feels to stand tall and proud on a rodeo platform, receive a purse and silver buckle, thousands of people shading their eyes to catch a glimpse. How it feels to be hobbled by clubs and rifle butts, and to live with God's anger at having cut open a Chinese soldier on a bleak Korean hillside, after vowing not to take another's life.

Joselito dreams out loud of the whores waiting in Walla Walla at The Ritz, The Waldorf, The Savoy, and talks of his home in Waco, his wife and children. He wonders if tonight he will feel the deep ache he has felt every night since the start of the peas, during the melons in Arizona, the beets in California, every night he has cried himself to sleep.

I lick my cracked lips and try to recall a summer free of dust and sweat, and dream of taking off for the beach in my '38 Ford with a soft-eyed girl, a bucket of Friar Tuck chicken and a short case of Miller's, laying a blanket on the cool sand at the mouth of the cave beside the waterfall at Hug Point.

Shadows widen as the day wears on. In the shade between viners, a thermometer registers one hundred and five degrees, the top mark on the tube. A mirage shatters as a truck lurches from the road and fishtails across the ocean of dust. Load follows load as the fat sun settles on the chalk-white horizon. Water from the tap, thick and foul, turns the tin cup brown.

I watch the last trucks of the dayshift drop their loads and drive off, trailing plumes of dust that hang like dirty gauze curtains in the late sun's glow. Turning, I take my pitchfork to the tangled vines. Springs groan, gears grumble as man-jack trucks bump over ruts between road and runway. Night-shift workers drop, choose partners, wait and watch as mechanics throw levers and idle the viners.

I join day workers at the door of a pickup where a straw boss thumbs through checks for ten dollars and thirty-one cents. I stamp my feet to separate caked mud from boot soles, slap dust from my shirt, and climb aboard a man-jack truck for the ride back to Athena.

We cash our checks and scatter. Doc and Luke head to the liquor store. Wilber hits Pike's Cafe, a swinging-door saloon even the town's tough cops skirt at night. Jamey leads a parade to the corner grocery. Joselito trudges off toward Walla Walla, wagging his thumb at a passing pickup. Bo Charlie heads for the hobo jungle around a bend in the tracks south of Rogers Brothers Cannery. Willy Democrat Jones heads for the truck barn to dance for his supper after wiring his pay to his mother.

Professor and I take stalls in the bathhouse across from Pike's, and later grab a bite at the Athena Hotel café, where I keep Hank Williams busy, five plays for a quarter, and Hank Snow: *I met a lit-tle Span-ish girl, down in La-ra-do....*

I drag my weary bones to the ten-by-twelve-foot cabin I rent for three dollars a week at the cannery work camp—military bunk, unfinished wood table and chair, naked light bulb dangling by a frayed cord—and settle in to capture the day on paper. Then the struggle to forget, so I might pass tomorrow's early hours as a stranger to the fields, the dust, the burning sun, the pain of skin rubbed raw by fireweed needles. But the digging-lifting-swinging drill penetrates even my dreams.

*
 * *

Epilogue

Joining me on the Preacher's truck the next morning were Bo Charlie, Joselito, Professor, and Willy Democrat Jones. Bo said he'd heard Doc and Luke had hopped a northbound freight, following their star to the Big Rock Candy Mountain.

Wilber kept two friends in drinks until his money ran out. He promised to get more. They told him if he didn't they'd kick his head in. I found him late that night, sprawled at the door to the camp lavatory, eyes puffed shut, nose plastered flat. He begged me for money to buy drinks for his friends.

Jamey entertained a cluster of winos with his Rose Bowl heroics, passing his clippings around with jugs of dago red.

He was found the following afternoon in the alley behind the bathhouse, circled by empties. Fire ants had eaten his eyes.

When the peas played out, I worked nightshift at Rogers Cannery for three weeks, wheeling racks of cans into retorts, mostly carrots and corn.

One moonless night the abandoned blacksmith shop two blocks east went up in flames. I wandered over on my lunch break, kicked over a smoldering mattress in the charred ruins to discover a rib cage and a skull blown wide open. Learned later it was the red-haired, freckle-faced kid from Oregon City I'd met a couple of weeks before.

College bound, I thumbed to Portland and caught the Blue Bus home to Lake Grove. Now when I dip into memory's well I see the Blue Mountains etched against a pale dawn sky, and breathe in the sweet aroma of crushed pea vines.

About the Author

David Hedges was born January 9, 1937 in Portland, Oregon, and spent his formative years in Portland and Lake Grove. He attended West Linn High School for one year, then transferred to the new Lake Oswego High, where he graduated in 1954.

He attended Oregon State College (now University) on a

Naval ROTC scholarship before dropping out, six months shy of a degree and a commission in the Navy. He spent those six months in New York City's Greenwich Village, hanging out at the White Horse Tavern, sitting in the chair Dylan Thomas had kept warm a few years before, and writing poetry. Returning to Oregon, he enrolled at Portland State College (now University) and graduated in 1959.

High school graduation photo, 1954

For the next 34 years, 11 of them as a freelance, he worked as a writer in the fields of journalism, public relations, advertising, and politics, winning numerous awards. He was twice named one of Oregon's "Ten Outstanding Young Men" for his long list of civic activities.

In 1993, he retired from commercial writing and divided his time between creative writing and environmental, political and social activism. When he ran for state representative in 2000, the Oregon League of Conservation Voters (OLCV) dubbed him an "environmental warrior" for his successful fight to save Canemah Bluff, above the Falls of the Willamette—a geologic, ecological, archaeological, cultural, and scenic wonder—from development as a subdivision.

His poems have appeared in *Poetry, Measure, Able Muse, Poet Lore, Light Quarterly, Light* (online), *Trinacria,* and *The Christian Science Monitor,* among others, and, closer to home, *Northwest Magazine, Left Bank, Calapooya Collage, Windfall, Bellowing Ark, Verseweavers,* and *Willamette Week.* His work is anthologized in *Stafford's Road, Portland Lights, All Said & Done (UK),* and others.

He is the author of *Petty Frogs on the Potomac* (1997), a satire in verse, and five chapbooks: *The Wild Bunch* (1998), *Brother Joe* (2000), *Steens Mountain Sunrise: Poems of the Northern Great Basin* (2004), *Selected Sonnets* (2006), and *A Funny Thing Happened on My Way to a Geology Degree* (Finishing Line Press, 2011).

He served on the board of the Oregon Poetry Association for twenty-four years, six as president and twelve as founding editor of *Verseweavers,* OPA's anthology of prize poems. He was a board member of the Portland Poetry Festival, and has served on the Oregon Cultural Heritage Commission board since 1988.

He co-founded, with State Librarian Jim Scheppke and Poet Laureate Lawson Inada, the Oregon Poetry Collection, now at the University of Oregon's Knight Library.

At the 2003 Oregon Book Awards, he received the Stewart H. Holbrook Literary Legacy Award for his contributions to the state's literary life.